ABSENTEEISM
IN INDUSTRY

Publication Number 969

AMERICAN LECTURE SERIES®

A Publication in

The BANNERSTONE DIVISION *of*
AMERICAN LECTURES IN COMMUNICATIONS

Editor

DOMINICK A. BARBARA, M.D.
Formerly, Head of the Speech Department
Karen Horney Clinic
New York, New York

ABSENTEEISM IN INDUSTRY

By

STANLEY F. YOLLES, M.D.

Professor and Chairman
Department of Psychiatry
Health Sciences Center
State University of New York at Stony Brook
Senior Consultant in Psychiatry
South Oaks Hospital

PASQUALE A. CARONE, M.D.

Medical Director
South Oaks Hospital (The Long Island Home, Ltd.)
Director of South Oaks Foundation
Amityville, New York
Associate Professor of Clinical Psychiatry
State University of New York at Stony Brook

LEONARD W. KRINSKY, Ph.D.

Director of Psychological Services
South Oaks Hospital (The Long Island Home, Ltd.)
Assistant Director of Research
South Oaks Foundation
Associate Professor of Clinical Psychiatry
State University of New York at Stony Brook

CHARLES C THOMAS • PUBLISHER
Springfield • Illinois • U.S.A.

Published and Distributed Throughout the World by

CHARLES C THOMAS • PUBLISHER

BANNERSTONE HOUSE

301-327 East Lawrence Avenue, Springfield, Illinois, U.S.A.

© *1975 by* CHARLES C THOMAS • PUBLISHER

ISBN 0-398-03302-1

Library of Congress Catalog Card Number: 74 12035

With THOMAS BOOKS *careful attention is given to all details of manufacturing and design. It is the Publisher's desire to present books that are satisfactory as to their physical qualities and artistic possibilities and appropriate for their particular use.* THOMAS BOOKS *will be true to those laws of quality that assure a good name and good will.*

Printed in the United States of America

N-1

Library of Congress Cataloging in Publication Data

Yolles, Stanley F. 1919-
    Absenteeism in industry

(American lecture series, publication no. 969 A publication in the Bannerstone division of American lectures in communications)

Based on papers presented at a conference sponsored by the South Oaks Foundation, in conjunction with the Dept. of Psychiatry, State University of New York at Stony Brook Apr. 5 and 6, 1973.

1. Absenteeism (Labor)—Congresses. 2. Absenteeism (Labor)—United States Congresses. I. Carone, Pasquale A., joint author. II. Krinsky, Leonard W., joint author. III. South Oaks Foundation. IV. New York (State). State University at Stony Brook Dept. of Psychiatry V. Title.

HD5115.Y64   658.31-22   74-12035

ISBN 0-398-03302-1

To our friends and colleagues who aided and encouraged us, and to those absent workers to whom we have dedicated ourselves . . .

CONTRIBUTORS

HAROLD A. ABRAMSON, M.D.
Director of Research
South Oaks Foundation

GEORGE J. ADLER, M.D.
Vice Chairman
Regional Representative
Education Commission
NYS Academy of
Family Physicians

PETER J. ANDRESAKIS
Employee Relations Manager
Doubleday & Company, Inc.

JOHN L. BARRY
Commissioner
Police Department
County of Suffolk

ALFRED BESUNDER, ESQ.
Director
NYS Mental Health Information Service
Second Judicial Department

CLEMENT J. BOCCALINI, M.D.
President Elect
N.Y.S. Academy of Family Physicians

LEONARD S. BRAHEN, Ph.D., M.D.
Director, Medical Research & Education
Department of Drug & Alcohol Addiction
County of Nassau

HERBERT P. BRANDT, M.D.
Commissioner
Department of Mental Health
County of Suffolk

vii

HENRY BRILL, M.D.
Director
Pilgrim State Hospital

THE HON. JACK J. CANNAVO
Judge
Family Court, State of New York
County of Suffolk

CAPT. PATRICK F. CARONE, M.D.
Department of Psychiatry
U.S. Army Hospital (Ky.)

THE HONORABLE RALPH G. CASO
Nassau County Executive

ANTHONY J. COSTALDO
Director, Community Services
L.I. Federation of Labor, AFL/CIO

TIMOTHY W. COSTELLO, Ph.D.
President
Adelphi University

ORMAN CROCKER
Executive Director
L.I. Council on Alcoholism

GORDON F. DERNER, Ph.D.
Dean and Professor
Institute of Advanced Psychological Studies
Adelphi University

MICHAEL O. DIAMOND
Coordinator
Employees' Assistance Unit
NYC Department of Sanitation

PAUL J. DONNELLY, JR., ESQ.
General Attorney
The Long Island Railroad

J. C. DUFFY, M.D.
Medical Director
International Business Machines Corp.

RONALD J. EDEEN
Director of Probation
County of Suffolk

ROBERT E. FISHBEIN, M.D.
Medical Director
Sperry Rand Corporation

MARK E. FOX, M.D.
Medical Director
The Long Island Railroad

LOUIS R. HOTT, M.D.
Medical Director
Karen Horney Clinic

ROBERT P. JESSUP, M.D.
Medical Director
Grumman Aerospace Corp.

J. L. KAULL
Manager, Manpower Development
Hazeltine Corporation

SHERMAN N. KIEFFER, M.D.
Professor and Vice-Chairman
Department of Psychiatry
Health Sciences Center
State University of N.Y. at Stony Brook

G. C. KITTS
Manager
Employee Benefits & Services
AIL, A Div. of Cutler-Hammer

THE HON. JOHN V. N. KLEIN
Suffolk County Executive

DANIEL KNOWLES
Director of Personnel
Grumman Aerospace Corporation

LEONARD W. KRINSKY, Ph.D.
Director
Psychological Services
South Oaks Hospital

SIDNEY LANG, ESQ.
Supervising Attorney
NYS Mental Health Information Service
Second Judicial Department

LOUIS A. LANZETTA, M.D.
Medical Director
NYC Transit Authority

WILLIAM F. LEE, JR., M.D.
Medical Director
General Foods Corporation

SANFORD V. LENZ
Regional Education Director
International Union of Electrical Workers

JOHN MacIVER, M.D.
Former Medical Director
United States Steel Corporation

EDWARD, H. MALONE, M.D.
Clinical Director
South Oaks Hospital

EILEEN D. McDERMOTT
Assistant Vice President
National Bank of North America

JOHN J. McMANUS
Assistant Director
Department of Community Services
AFL/CIO

SIDNEY MERLIS M.D.
Director of Psychiatric Research
Central Islip State Hospital

ROBERT S. MILLEN, M.D.
Medical Director
New York Stock Exchange

MORTON G. MILLER, M.D.
Associate Professor
Department of Psychiatry
Health Sciences Center
State University of New York
at Stony Brook

JOSEPH MORSELLO, Ph.D.
Associate Director
Psychological Services
South Oaks Hospital

WILLIAM J. NEENAN
Counselor
New York Life Insurance Co.

EDMUND C. NEUHAUS, Ph.D.
Director
The Rehabilitation Institute

ROBERT J. OEHRIG, M.D.
Medical Director
Home Life Insurance Company

MELVILLE G. ROSEN, M.D.
Professor, Dept. of Family Medicine
Health Sciences Center
State University of N.Y.
at Stony Brook

FREDERICK E. SNYDER, Ph.D.
Georgetown Law Center

JESSIE L. STEINFELD, M.D.
Surgeon General
U.S. Department of Health, Education
and Welfare

DONALD J. STRAIT
Vice President and General Manager
Fairchild Industries, Inc.

DANIEL J. SULLIVAN, M.D.
Associate Medical Director
Metropolitan Life Insurance Co.

PETER SWEISGOOD
Assistant Executive Director
L.I. Council on Alcoholism

HARRY E. TEBROCK, M.D.
Medical Director
General Telephone & Electronics Corp.

GRANVILLE I. WALKER, Jr., M.D.
Medical Director
The Chase Manhattan Bank

EILEEN WATERS, R.N.
Medical Department
National Bank of North America

H. R. WEISS Ph.D.
Chief, Psychology Service
Brooklyn VA Hospital

FREDERICK A. WHITEHOUSE, Ed.D.
Professor of Education
Coordinator, Rehabilitation
Counselor Training Program
Hofstra University

STANLEY F. YOLLES, M.D.
Professor & Chairman
Department of Psychiatry
Health Sciences Center
State University of N.Y.
at Stony Brook

SIDNEY ZUCKERMAN, M.D.
Medical Director
Sperry Division
Sperry Rand Corporation

PREFACE

O N April the fifth and sixth, 1973, South Oaks Foundation, in conjunction with the Department of Psychiatry, School of Medicine, State University of New York at Stony Brook, sponsored a conference on *Absenteeism in Industry*.

Concerned over the fact that, too often, absenteeism has been considered as either a symptom or an impersonal condition affecting industrial profits, the conference sponsors arranged for an intensive examination of the reasons for absenteeism from a variety of points of view.

This volume is the synthesis of those viewpoints, including as it does panel discussions that resulted from comments by industrial psychologists, labor representatives, industrial executives, family physicians, public officials, personnel directors, and psychiatrists.

These discussions exemplify an awareness of the comprehensive scope of industrial problems, of which absenteeism, of itself, is only one symptom. The discussions further indicate some initial efforts—on the part of everyone involved—to substitute cooperative endeavors for the traditional adversary stance of labor and management.

It is not surprising that the problem remains unresolved. No two-day conference can do much more than set the stage for future considerations and further discussion. However, because it established the existence of many common denominators, among the various groups represented in the consideration of absenteeism, the conference was successful in establishing a framework for cooperation, as a change from traditional separatism.

These discussions are exploratory; they provide information and keys to attitudinal "sets" which should be of benefit to anyone concerned with individual and corporate social problems of the times.

Stanley F. Yolles
Pasquale A. Carone
Leonard W. Krinsky

xiii

INTRODUCTION

There is much to be said for absence—it makes the heart grow fonder
—and out of sight out of mind—we meet here today not so much to
talk about absence but what is more important, presence (part of the
introductory remarks)

PASQUALE A. CARONE

THIS BOOK IS CONCERNED with the psychiatric/psychological aspects of absenteeism. In defining this goal we purposely did not concern ourselves with the number of employees who have legitimate medical reasons for not being on the job. This constitutes a great deal of the absenteeism in American industry and is unavoidable. Our task was to concern ourselves with those workers who stay off the job because of other reasons. It is estimated by some investigators that this type of absenteeism costs our country many billions of dollars yearly.

There are questions raised and divergent opinions expressed as to how absenteeism should be treated. Should the employee be discharged for excessive absence? Should the company hire a mental health team to deal with such problems? Should a social worker be employed who will enter the home of the employee to learn more of the intrapsychic dynamics? Is it the sole province of the unions and labor movement to deal with absenteeism? Can fear and the setting of overly stringent standards result in less absenteeism, or does this create more of a problem? Can the personnel department of a company and its management institute programs to reduce this major problem? Does the family doctor and the fact that he may often write excuses add undue expenses to the cost of running a company? And, lastly, what can government do in the resolution of this ongoing major dilemna? These are questions which are raised, answered in part, and at times left unanswered for the reader to arrive at his own opinion.

The first group of papers focus on the roles of labor, management and the industrial psychologist. Motivational techniques are discussed at length. There seems to be a conflict between industry, which feels the need to set performance standards, and labor, which appears to be more concerned with the overall welfare of the worker. The personnel director often seems to stand between two extremes, while the industrial psychologist searches for techniques which will concomitantly aid the worker and the company.

The second group of papers concerns itself with the medical/psychiatric viewpoint. The incidence of undetected mental illness is explored. The need for a mental health team in a large corporation is discussed with both its pros and cons. The family doctor is seen as an integral cog in the overall treatment program. The constructive ways in which a family physician can operate are a part of this book and there is also some discussion of the abuses. The Surgeon General discusses very important statistics and there is an extensive description of the way in which cigarette smoking is a factor.

The purpose of this conference was both to educate and to communicate. It is hoped that all who participated learned that new ideas and new concepts must be instituted and constantly evaluated. It is only by an overall attack on the problem from all sectors involved with workers that some resolution of this major problem can be effected.

ACKNOWLEDGMENTS

PREPARATION OF A BOOK SUCH as this involves not only the authors but many others who work long hours and lend their talents. This book represents the end product of one of the South Oaks Hospital/State University of New York at Stony Brook annual conferences. These conferences are held in the spring of each year and are devoted to problems in psychiatric medicine. The preparations, of course, began many months earlier.

This book could not have come to fruition without the co-operation of all speakers and panelists. Each made an individual contribution at the meetings and in the editing of this volume.

We are deeply indebted to the Board of Directors of South Oaks Hospital for their recognizing the need for an overall attack on problems of psychiatric medicine. They have actively supported us in all ways in this endeavor.

At South Oaks we are also deeply indebted to our Executive Assistant, Mrs. Catherine Martens, and to our Director of Public Relations, Mrs. Lynn Black.

We could not have proceeded without the guidance, patience, and expertise of our publisher, Mr. Payne E L Thomas. He, along with our editor, Dominick A. Barbara, M.D., were available for guidance and support.

Lastly, our thanks to our editorial assistant, Mrs. Susan K. Lattin. She helped us meet deadlines and served as a constant prod to the authors in bringing this volume to fruition.

CONTENTS

ABSENTEEISM
IN INDUSTRY

THE INDUSTRIAL PSYCHOLOGIST LOOKS AT ABSENTEEISM

Timothy W. Costello*

— — — — — — — — — — — — — — —

ABSENTEEISM MIGHT BEST BE defined as one symptom of the individual's total adjustment to the job situation. (Perhaps the single most sensitive measure of morale is rate of absenteeism.) There is a need here to differentiate between the long-term absence resulting from serious illness and the short-term absences distributed over the year which are largely discretionary and a result of forces which will be discussed later.

One's adjustment to a job can be expressed along a continuum that ranges from creative productivity (going beyond the routine demands of the job) to discontinuing membership in the organization (actually leaving the job). Between these extremes is a number of symptoms expressing varied degrees of adjustment; these include accident rate, number of personal grievances, rate of tardiness, and rate of absenteeism. It is important to note that these behavioral expressions may be the result not only of the individual's adjustment to the job, but of other factors as well. There are some accidents and absences that are simply beyond the individual's control. The kinds of industrial problems with which we are dealing here, however, are not those which occur under uncontrollable circumstances, but those which are subject to the relationships between society, management, and the em-

---

*Dr. Timothy Costello is an industrial psychologist who holds a doctorate in psychology from Fordham University. A Diplomate of the American Board of Professional Psychology, he served on the faculty of New York University for twenty-one years and then became Deputy Mayor of New York City. There he directed a staff of 150 management scientist analysts and researchers. Dr. Costello is now President of Adelphi University, Garden City, New York.

ployee. These are the types of problems affected by our demands
and then alleviated by modification of those demands.

Factors that affect the rate of absenteeism can be grouped
under three headings along with a set of approaches to be used
in dealing with the problem. Absenteeism is first affected by the
attitude of the total society toward presence at work. Just as the
rate of drug usage is seen as an expression of society's acceptance
of chemistry as a way of adjusting to life, so society's general attitude toward presence on the job truly has an effect on absenteeism.

As an employment phenomenon, absenteeism has increased
over the past twenty years, largely as a result of two characteristics
of the total society during this period of time. First of all, work
has become a much less central value in the lives of individuals
in our society; work is seen as only one way in which the individual's ego is expressed, as only one of the principal sources of
satisfaction. It is no longer so central a value of our society that
the adult male or female will occupy his productive hours almost
exclusively with on-the-job performance.

The productive use of leisure time has become almost as important; being present on the job, creatively occupied, is no longer
so vital a part of the individual's personal adjustment. There are
so many additional ways of being creative than coming to work
in the morning; the "do-it-yourself" vogue which has captured
America is one such expression. Even professionals now take pride
in doing the household plumbing. Males are finding creative out-
lets in artistic endeavors, and golf has become almost an occupation among a segment of our society.

There are many socially approved and ego-satisfying things
that a grown individual can do today. They can be as valuable
to him in holding on to his sense of self-esteem and dignity as
working successfully on the job. Of course, this is not true for
everyone; there are still many individuals for whom work is the
central value in life.

It is tempting to sort people into two categories: those for
whom job activity is central to the way in which their personalities
and daily activities are organized, and those for whom work is a
necessary evil required to earn income. Clearly, absenteeism will

be much higher for that group for whom work is a necessary evil.

The second characteristic of the total society that seems to have a direct impact on absenteeism is the whole system of cues that tell the individual that the goal is to be off the job as much as possible. The rewards we offer individuals in the employment situation are increased opportunities to be away from the job; the system that an organization has available to influence and shape the behavior of the individual continues to emphasize how little time has to be spent on the job. Looking at the fringe benefit package over the past twenty years shows that vacation time has increased and daily hours have been reduced. In addition, management offers stated coffee breaks, extended lunch hours, and built-in guaranteed sick leave; furthermore, the age of mandatory retirement has been lowered. Absenteeism, then, is simply a relatively illegitimate way of conforming with society's expression of the notion that successful people have more time off the job than on the job. The reward system states that the better one's performance is, the more often one can stay off the job; so the individual conforms. He moves toward those job opportunities where there is abundant vacation, few hours to work, many breaks during the day, guaranteed sick leave, and where he can also take absences at will. Steps that we take to reduce absences must deal to some extent with the factors in the larger society that affect the attitudes that people bring to the work scene.

Another basic factor affecting the rate of absenteeism involves what actually happens on the job. At this point, a definition of what we mean by "organization" is in order since absenteeism always occurs in relation to some organization. It is possible to view an organization as a profit-making or service-rendering structure, but this idea does not help us to understand the absenteeism problem. From a manager's point of view, an organization is a problem-solving system, one that allocates resources and assigns those resources in an effort to solve problems identified as goals of the organization. In general, the extent to which the organization is an efficient and effective problem-solving system dictates the extent to which absenteeism is minimized.

It is more important in a discussion of absenteeism to see the organization as a social system providing for accommodation or adjustment among a variety of human members of that system. This can be described as a process of fusion with a two-way flow of influence. The organization expresses its energy (within the context of its own personality around a set of goals) by specifying job descriptions that become activities for individuals. The individual who enters this organization also expresses a flow of influence in expression of his own energy; he is driven to maximize or optimize his goals. Here the two forces come together. When there is a high degree of fusion between the expression of the organization's energies and those of the individual, there is a maximum degree of goal achievement for both sides. In such a setting, absenteeism would be extremely low.

For this reason, any approach to discretionary absenteeism must look at the degree to which the individual finds satisfaction in the nature of his work. Specific factors within this general area include job content. Many of today's jobs are much less satisfying activities than they may have been in the past. As we have moved increasingly towards mass production and have sought the aid of nonhuman power to solve the problems of the organization, we have reduced the amount the individual himself can contribute to the solution of a problem. Despite what was said earlier about work being less of a central value, still important to the lives of most individuals is their capacity to solve problems and contribute solutions to the environment in which they exist.

The extent to which an organization narrows the individual's opportunities to make significant contributions has a constricting effect on the meaningfulness of the job for that individual. As a result, there is less reason for him to worry about whether or not to report for work each day. We have so structured jobs, have become so scientific about the way we get our work done, and are so unwilling to take chances that we have effectively narrowed the zone of freedom that surrounds a job for the individual. At that point there is no longer a challenge and the employee does not feel that it makes much difference to the organization whether he is there or not. It only makes a difference if there is someone who is concerned about the employee's presence on the job. This factor will have an impact on the kind of approach to take when dealing with absenteeism due to dissatisfaction with job content.

A second characteristic under the general heading of nature of the work is the technical nature of the operation. The degree to which the individual is prepared to deal with the technical process, the amount of training that he has been given to deal with situations that may come up, is an important factor in overall adjustment to the work situation. As narrowly as we have circumscribed the individual's behaviors at work, there are still aspects of the job that arouse anxiety. The less well trained an employee is, the less secure he feels to deal with job problems and the more likely it is that he will occasionally choose to stay home rather than come into work.

There are many other technical aspects of the job that affect absenteeism in different organizations. The noisier the job is, the more polluted the environment, and the more chaotic the work scene, the more pressures there are on the individual to avoid the entire situation and not to come to work.

Aside from the content and technical nature of the job, it is important to consider the social aspects. In general, the more effectively trained a man's supervisor is, the less likely it is that social tensions will develop and lead to absenteeism. Criticism of the individual's work, an embarrassment on the job, or a lack of understanding between fellow workers can increase the likelihood that a given employee will not appear for work the next morning. Supervisory training, or human relations training, is definitely in order to avoid that sort of situation.

The third major factor contributing to absenteeism involves characteristics of the individual employee. Included in this category are the absentee-prone individuals, those who have learned to adjust to life's tensions by withdrawing and staying away. A refined measure of attendance at the individual's last school would probably be as predictive of his absence rate as any other measure. A life-style resulting in frequent discretionary absences is a form of the problem confined to a relatively small percentage of the work force. There is not very much an organization can do to affect this facet of an individual's life-style critically. If early childhood patterns have led to that kind of an adjustment, no matter how attractive the work situation is made and no matter what is done to change the centrality of work in the individual's life, the absentee problem will remain.

There are, of course, many psychiatric characteristics influencing absenteeism. Alcoholism is one of the principal factors affecting irregular expressions of absenteeism. Other forms of psychiatric maladjustment contribute to absenteeism as well.

Another characteristic of the employee himself contributing to absenteeism is proneness to psychosomatic illnesses. In this context, a psychosomatic ailment is any physical symptom that serves a psychological value for the individual. While a cold may be an expression of a legitimate virus that is present, the individual who uses this cold to stay away from work is relying on a psychosomatic illness. If he goes to work, however, it is a physical illness. As long as there is some choice in the matter (I am not speaking of totally disabled individuals) the ailment is psychosomatic when the individual chooses to remain away from work. There is a whole series of psychosomatic ailments covered up by very legitimate physical illnesses for which the individual receives legitimate sympathy and legitimate treatment but which he uses also as an excuse for staying away from work.

Finally, in the life patterns of many employees there are inconveniences or handicaps as a result of peculiar problems of family living or of location that add to absenteeism. For example, mothers who work always have the problem of being concerned about sick children. Increasingly, we are beginning to recognize that day care is a responsibility of the employer if we are to give women full opportunities at careers. Simple problems of transportation or of caring for poorly equipped houses or apartments are characteristics of the individual's personal living pattern that can interfere with his ability to get to work.

I have attempted to list the principal sources of discretionary absenteeism in an organization. What approaches can be taken to do something about this? I mentioned that the approaches must relate to the three principal forces affecting absenteeism: the larger environment, the organization environment, and the personal characteristics of the employee himself.

I feel that society is adjusting to work, not so much by increasing the individual's desire to work, but rather by building into the work pattern the opportunity for planned absences. That is one approach to dealing with the effect absenteeism has on organizational performance. An unpredicted absence is a more handicapping occurrence than a predicted one. Management can struggle against the tide of social value and try to encourage employees to come into work every day, or the individual can be notified that he has a certain number of sick days, enabling him to signal in advance certain occasions when he will be absent. In that way, management can accommodate for the absence, organizing the work force accordingly. This is not a solution to the problem, but it does minimize the effect.

approach to it

Involved in this approach might be the introduction of a counterincentive. Employees who do not use their allotted days of sick leave may exchange them on some basis such as terminal leave or financial renumeration at the end of the year. In effect, this is reversing the trend; the reward system now encourages job attendance in an indirect fashion. The important point is that it is extremely difficult to work upstream against values that so prize staying away from the job. Better planning is the best solution. *1st adjust to d – planned absences*

A second major approach to the absenteeism problem has to do with the social health of the organization itself. The degree to which the work structure allows enlargement of the role of the individual in the organization will reduce absenteeism. Anything that increases the individual's freedom to make decisions about his work, as well as anything that raises the level of supervisory performance affects the rate of absenteeism. In addition, increasing the skill the individual has in performing his job increases his total adjustment to that situation and to some extent reduces the pressures keeping him away from his job. Smoothing over the technical aspects of the job that are unpleasant to the individual is also important. (This might include the introduction of pleasant music, reducing overall noise level, and generally ordering the work situation so that it is less chaotic.) Involving employees by

2

requesting their opinions about the work situation, conducting morale surveys, and providing regular training opportunities pay off in dollars in terms of reduced absenteeism.

Very frequently when we speak of absenteeism we talk about it in terms of programs for controlling the problem. What sanctions can an organization employ to reduce absenteeism? I have already identified what I believe to be the most powerful weapons for control. Anything beyond that will have minimal impact. Can we punish the absentee? The only punishment that works (and this may have such side effects that it may be better not to utilize it) is to fire the frequently absent and irresponsible individual after appropriate warnings and within the personnel plan of the organization.

The final approach to the problem is to train supervisors to tactfully and sensitively make every individual aware that they know he was absent. The supervisor should convey the impression that it is important to him that the employee not be absent. A fining system or reduction in pay, anything that has punitive aspects to it, will in the long run produce more negative side effects than good. Letting the individual know that his absence was important to his superiors and to his peers on the job seems to be a more effective approach.

DISCUSSION

Panelists in this discussion were experts in the fields of psychology and industrial problems. They included *Gordon F. Derner,* Ph.D., Dean and Professor, Institute of Advanced Psychological Studies, Adelphi University; *Sanford V. Lenz,* Regional Educational Director, International Union of Electrical Workers; and *Joseph Morsello,* Ph.D., Associate Director of Psychological Services, South Oaks Hospital. Others included *Edmund C. Neuhaus,* Ph.D., Director, The Rehabilitation Institute; *Peter Sweisgood,* Assistant Executive Director, The Long Island Council on Alcoholism; and *H. R. Weiss,* Ph.D., Chief, Psychology Service, Brooklyn V. A. Hospital.

Dr. Weiss:

In considering absenteeism, there are many questions that

need to be answered. First of all, how do we go about making early identification of absenteeism among our employees? Can we use the same techniques that we use to identify the alcohol and drug abuser? In addition, we must learn to recognize the factors that lead to increased severity of the problem. We must keep chronological records that enable us not only to accurately identify that chronically absent employee but which also enable our supervisors to have some understanding of what absenteeism means. Dealing with absenteeism requires starting at the beginning. Large organizations should try to identify the potential supervisor early in his development and offer him training in recognizing mental health problems like absenteeism.

We must change the things we use to motivate employees. Reward should be used in place of punishment. Furthermore, rewards do not always have to be monetary in nature. Prestige and recognition can also be used successfully to motivate employees.

Mr. Sweisgood:

The possibility of alcoholism should not be overlooked for any employee whose attendance record is suspect. Managers should keep careful records of attendance and performance and should speak to employees who have been absent. If a pattern of absenteeism emerges, the employee should be sent to the medical department and from there to the Council on Alcoholism if the need is indicated.

Dr. Neuhaus:

I am a founder and director of a vocational rehabilitation facility. Our goal has been to train and place emotionally disturbed individuals who have left the hospital environment and enable them to get ready for competitive employment.

The most prevalent reason I have heard for not going to work comes from young people who do not like work because "it really has no meaning; work has no challenge." When questioned further, these individuals reflect on the values of today's society; they do not want simply to be dispensable cogs in the much larger machinery of society.

People who are concerned with maintaining employment make

the repeated observation that there is something basically wrong with our materialistic, technological society. Paul Goodman, author of *Growing Up Absurd,* pointed out that we are preparing our youth for jobs that really have false appeals, that have an inherent sense of uselessness about them. There is a great deal of hypocrisy in our society.

There is still another point to consider when dealing with absenteeism. A work relationship is basically an authority relationship. The way an individual has learned to cope with authority and the kind of authority he meets in his life will effect how he relates on the job and how happy he is on the job. It has generally been found that many people become quite unhappy under the authoritative type of supervisor. Too often, the authoritarian approach is dehumanizing.

Rollo May once wrote, "Man does not live by the clock alone." The significance of the time one spends in any kind of activity is what is really important, not the amount of time. Work can be meaningful, but we must attempt to change society's values.

Dr. Derner:

Absenteeism based on job dissatisfaction is something which demands our attention. It is fallacious to suggest that we can keep our enthusiasm up for any length of time by shouting, "Get in there and keep punching!" After a while, people begin to ask for what are they trying so hard, and instead of being cooperative they become resistant.

If we are going to "humanize" jobs, then we must consider the human being's aspirations, fears, pleasures, desires, needs frustrations, and anger. In order for a job to be worthwhile, employees must have a feeling of self-respect.

If we want to determine the causes of absenteeism, we must look at the individual who is absent. One explanation, of course, is alcoholism, and this problem must be dealt with from several different viewpoints including that of the use of the psychologist.

Mr. Lenz:

I represent labor's view of absenteeism. The problem is simple. It has to do with the fact that the industrial psychologist's point of view, the managers' point of view, and the company president's point of view always seem to focus on the victim and then blame him. It strikes me that we have all been looking at the worker as a worker. Apparently, nothing else about him concerns us.

Absenteeism is a very serious problem because it results in decreased productivity. It strikes me that the last person in the world to whom I would want to tell my personal problems is the man who can give me my raises, can hire and fire me, and can affect my day-to-day work assignments. My livelihood, my ability to bring home a salary, is directly affected by what the supervisor thinks and knows about me.

In today's society, confidentiality has all but disappeared. The employee's privacy is invaded to an amazing extent by people who claim to be helping him. Today, no employee willingly discusses his personal, family, or financial problems with his supervisor.

The problem that seems most relevant to absenteeism is that everyone's approach to the worker has been in the direction of change. Everyone wants to change the worker into what someone else wants him to be. The objectives of industry's leaders are productivity and profit. The well-being of the employee is only secondary. If our objective in discussing absenteeism is to change the employee to fit industry's profit motive, we will never come to a solution.

As a union official, my concern is the well-being of my membership. The right man to be trained in industrial psychology is not the supervisor. It is the shop steward. Our experience with alcoholism has shown that such cases are best served by union stewards who work closely with management to develop alcoholism programs. The steward can maintain close contact with the troubled employee. The peer knowledge of circumstance is at least the first step toward understanding and helping an employee. By breaking the peer relationship and expecting someone in a supervisor position to help the employee, industry moves backwards instead of forwards.

The pressure on the supervisor is not such that his primary concern is the well-being of the individual. The well-being of the employee might be important to the supervisor for his other purposes. The fact remains, however, that the employee's happiness is not his prime function.

A factory without a union needs someone who fills the function of the shop steward. An ombudsman is appropriate in most cases. A company needs someone whose responsibility is not production, who is concerned for the employee, who can say to the employee, "Productivity and profits are important, but first we need you. Is there something we can do to help you?" That is the primary objective of unions, and that is the approach we must use if we are ever to solve industrial problems.

Dr. Morsello:

As a clinical psychologist who deals with many severely disturbed people, I see the causes of absenteeism on two levels, one external to and one within the individual.

External factors leading to absenteeism include the work environment, which may or may not be conducive to individuals being present. Work circumstances are often lacking; they do not fulfill basic human needs such as respect and recognition. The work environment is often a boring one, and finally, there are occasionally too many pressures bearing on employees.

Internal dynamics, unrecognized by employers, frequently contribute to absenteeism. The internal state of anxiety or depression can easily be aggravated by external circumstances, and the result is absenteeism. Mental health experts are needed in industry to deal with such situations, and supervisors must be taught to look objectively at the environment they are building for employees to work in.

Dr. Weiss:

As an example of the use of positive incentives for coming to work, the federal government is now enabling its employees to accumulate sick leave over years. As far as can be determined, this practice has had a minimal impact on rates of absenteeism. It is only after the individual has decided to remain on the job for at least half of his active working years that he begins to recognize the benefits of accumulating sick leave in terms of unexpected illnesses and retirement.

Audience:

The average person does not have the opportunity to work at the job of his choice. He has to take whatever job his qualifications happen to fit. This is why so many employees are unhappy. It is primarily in the blue collar population that this happens.

Mr. Lenz:

This is very true. Too often, we focus on the upper middle class when we discuss industrial health problems. It is the working poor who have the real problems, however. Many of these individuals are in a continual state of fatigue because they hold two jobs, their wives hold one, and their children must be taken care of. Their financial problems are not those of how to pay for their next vacation trip, but how to pay the rent and food bills.

Audience:

This difference between the middle-class and lower-class employees relates to the value of the shop steward. The middle-class person who has a problem will go to a psychologist or psychiatrist. The lower class employee is not only financially unable to go to a private mental health expert, but feels very threatened by even a company psychologist and is therefore very reluctant to go to such a professional. He is much more prone to go to and relate to a peer, the shop steward. It is important, however, to make sure that the shop stewards use professional back-up sources when dealing with troubled employees.

Dr. Morsello:

The shop steward can clearly be effective in the work situation. However, not every shop steward is capable of counselling employees. Furthermore, there is no longer a stigma attached to seeking the help of a psychologist, psychiatrist, or psychiatric social worker. Employees may be initially reluctant to seek such aid, but they quickly become acclimated to the idea.

Mr. Lenz:

I agree with both of these viewpoints. First of all, I did not mean to imply that a shop steward, by virtue of his elected position, is suddenly qualified to be a family counsellor. That is nonsense. I firmly believe that such an individual needs training. The training is not at a professional level, but makes him an expert at referral. Shop stewards are trained to notice symptoms, to offer initial intake counselling, to know what resources are available, and to make referrals. Once the troubled employee is in the hands of the professional, he does accept the help of the professional and is not reluctant to ask for help.

Our problem is to get the employee to the professional in the first place. This requires peer intake counselling with black community workers in black communities, Spanish-speaking community workers in the Spanish communities, and so on. Such counselling is not likely to come from a supervisor. The supervisor is clearly of a different class within the plant, is an authoritative and dangerous force in the eyes of the employee, and finally, is less likely to understand the world of the worker in a social sense.

Question:

It has been found that alcoholics respond much more to authoritative, job jeopardy situations than to understanding, sympathetic approaches. Are you not overlooking this evidence in the approach of shop stewards?

Mr. Lenz:

When we train shop stewards, one of the first warnings we give them is that they are not to be sympathetic and pitying, they are not to "cover up" employees' problems or underestimate the seriousness of problems like alcoholism. In the case of the alcoholic, the shop steward takes an authoritarian position and threatens the employee with job loss. The only place for the employee to go is to Alcoholics Anonymous. The union is *not* a place for the alcoholic to hide.

Question:

There have been many suggestions as to why people stay away from work. To what extent are these diagnoses of absenteeism based on talking with workers and to what extent are they based upon your own impressions? Work that seems boring or repetitive to a professional may not seem that way to the employee. Perhaps not all people are interested in challenging jobs.

Mr. Sweisgood:

Almost all of the conclusions as to why employees do not report for work are based on actual employee feedback.

Dr. Weiss:

We are finding more and more that many of our young people never developed good work habits, never developed positive attitudes toward work. It has been suggested that young people show a great deal of absenteeism because they have never really had to work. Work, however, is not the panacea for all of life's problems. We must think in terms of the kinds of creative activities that we can help people to learn. Unfortunately, many of present day technological advances tend to interfere with the work programs that young people would like to engage in. We are presently going through a transition period in which resistance is beginning to make itself felt in many aspects of work life.

In reviewing recent hospital management publications, I have found that there is a consistent, significantly higher percentage of absenteeism for women who hold hospital jobs. Women are clearly not receiving support in the way of day care and in the way of equality of help from husbands. Women are still perceived in demeaning roles. This creates the conflict that surfaces as absenteeism as an expression of rebellion against the male authority who so frequently has a top job.

Mr. Lenz:

I would like to address myself to the issue of job satisfaction. It is often said that the professional has a satisfying job because his work is so challenging, while the assembly line worker is bored to death because of the repetitious nature of his job. When it comes right down to it, however, the job satisfactions of the professional are essentially the right to be absent on the job. It is the right to sit around the office and talk, the right to take a slightly longer lunch "hour" than anyone else, the right to run personal errands during the day while blue collar workers must wait until Saturday. In fact, challenges are few and far between for the professional. Job satisfaction is the right to not spend the entire work day on the job.

The work environment for both the professional and the blue collar worker is a society in which people interrelate with each other. Their roles within that society may very well be satisfying without having anything to do with the specific work they do. Assembly line employees work with their hands; their minds and their tongues may very well be engaged in something else all day long, something very interesting, and something very satisfying. Things such as baseball pools, bowling teams, and company gossip are what make everyday work satisfying for employees.

If we are going to approach the issue of job satisfaction we must stop focusing on the employee as nothing but a worker and on his work environment as nothing but the work he does. We must look at life at work as a total environment instead of only studying what a worker does as his job. The important point is that some workers can enjoy repetitive work provided that there are other kinds of satisfactions for them on the job.

Dr. Neuhaus:

I cannot agree with that theory entirely. In my experience, employees explain their absenteeism as resulting from boredom and feelings of worthlessness: "This work has no meaning for me. There is a uselessness about what I am doing."

Dr. Derner:

In the 1960's, Swedish automobile factories created a new work environment. They let workers choose their own rates of production and choose their own jobs. The whole factory was redesigned so that employees could work on small teams and put an entire automobile together without any assembly line techniques.

The statistics show that this has not only increased economic efficiency, but has also cut down absentee rates significantly. The principle is one of greater worker participation and more meaningful work. I feel that this is further proof of Mr. Lenz's theory. The Swedish approach brings people together in such a way that they are now able to talk together during the day and share their thoughts. It may not be the building of a whole car that is exciting. Instead, it may be the opportunity to spend the day with peers that is enjoyable. It is possible that workers require a constant environment and homogeneous groupings to be satisfied on the job.

Dr. Weiss:

What is really being referred to is the Hawthorne effect. Psychologists have known for years that irrespective of how you change the work conditions and make work more novel and stimulating, it is the attention that workers respond to. When workers are recognized as people and participate in planning and decision making, they respond. When workers are treated as cogs in a machine, they respond as cogs do; they require frequent oiling and often go out of operation.

Mr. Lenz:

The Hawthorne effect is simply that if you look at any group of people as a group and change their circumstances, the mere fact that you looked at them makes them feel special, and they respond. The important point made in the Swedish factories was that the employees putting cars together worked effectively as a team. The team decided each day who would perform each function and who would act as foreman. Their societal relationship was more important than the fact that they were working in a different setting. The Hawthorne effect was not at work in this case. The workers now had the opportunity to interact with one another during actual working hours.

Audience:

I believe that most absenteeism today is due to younger (under thirty years old) employees. Older employees started work under a different set of standards and under a different economic situation and therefore have generally better attendance records. Absenteeism among younger employees is greater because in many cases management has not come across with a good human relations approach on a supervisory level. If we try to give today's younger workers direct orders without encouraging job participation, we will alienate them. This is just what has been done, and this encourages young employees to miss more work.

Dr. Derner:

It is the industrial psychologist's job to supply help to people who are absent because of personal or organizational problems. Professionals are needed to look at the organization in which the person works and to look at the person as a worker and as a human being under various pressures.

Chapter 2

THE INDUSTRIAL EXECUTIVE
LOOKS AT ABSENTEEISM

DONALD J. STRAIT*

THOSE OF US in industrial management positions today know a great deal about training men to do various jobs. There is a great deal that we do not know, however, about how to encourage these men to return to their jobs day after day. In some instances, the jobs may not be exciting or dynamic; in other cases, jobs may simply be non-meaningful to the men doing them. This chapter seeks to discuss what management can do to effectively analyze the absenteeism problem and to project certain practical approaches to reduce absenteeism to acceptable levels.

It takes a great deal of effort to really understand the complexities of absenteeism. It is a very subtle and sometimes an extremely elusive concept. Absenteeism is an amorphous problem; it is often difficult to pinpoint what percentage is avoidable or preventable.

Many studies have been undertaken to determine the patterns of absenteeism in particular facilities. The common factor demonstrated in these studies relates to management and supervision. What is important is the extent to which management can humanize jobs and make them more appealing, to add zest, to add interest to the jobs, and to try to create a competitive atmosphere within the organization so that the needs of the division can best be met in whatever products it is trying to produce.

---

*Donald J. Strait has had a distinguished career in the military and an equally eminent position in the field of industry. He flew in active combat in World War II, earning many decorations and achieving the rank of Major General; he served as Assistant Chief of Staff for the Department of Defense of the State of New Jersey. Upon leaving the service, Mr. Strait became Vice-President and General Manager of the Fairchild Republic Facility, Fairchild Industries, Inc.

As an example of this type of atmosphere, I turn to my own experience. When the aircraft division of my company was called upon to compete for an Air Force contract, the employees who were to be involved in this special project were set apart and given special prestige. These employees had a sense of pride about the project they were working on. Another example of added job interest is the weekly newsletter circulated throughout the plant and even sent home to employees who may be ill. There are also quarterly orientation meetings which include question-and-answer and "gripe" sessions.

Absenteeism is an unscheduled day off, whether for illness, bad weather, or a variety of personal reasons, ranging from hangovers to a decision to go fishing. There has certainly been a surge in the rate of absenteeism in the United States, and it has clearly become a growing concern to business. At some companies, the absentee problem is reaching a critical level. On a national scale, absenteeism has risen from about 4.3 percent in 1967 to over 5 percent in 1973.

Many people feel that one of the factors behind the increased absenteeism in industry is the growth of automation in assembly line techniques. This produces a lack of challenge in the worker's job and an absence of satisfaction in a job well done. In a factory in which a weapon system or major aircraft components are being built, a certain amount of automation is necessary. It is possible, however, to make a man's job interesting in spite of the automation. One of the things that has been successful in my own experience is that each employee know exactly how much he must produce on a given day. His performance and his ability to meet this standard is measured periodically, and the standard is steadily increased. As the employee becomes more adept and more professional, his supervisor begins to ask more of him. In this way, the employee is kept somewhat excited and more aggressively interested in what he is doing. Occasionally, it becomes necessary to lower the standard slightly or to place the individual in another position if it felt that he can be more productive in another area.

There is a new breed of workers in our factories today. Most of these people are better educated and more sensitive to discipline.

Many of these employees are young people who did not feel the effects of the great depression; they are not so concerned about job security. Instead, they are concerned that their basic needs are fulfilled and are, therefore, examining critically the worth of their jobs. The Gallup poll has shown a slow, steady decline in job satisfaction. Ten years ago, 90 percent of those questioned said that they were happy in their work. In 1972, just 83 percent gave positive responses.

A University of Michigan study found that disenchantment was highest among younger workers. Only about one third of the young employees questioned claimed that they were content with their jobs, while two thirds of the workers over fifty-five years old said they were satisfied. Recently, we found that young people want to start immediately in managerial positions. They do not want to start at the lowest level of a job area and learn the job completely before moving upward. Because of this attitude we have lost many young, promising engineers.

Absenteeism is a symptom of a deeper illness. Worker unrest is beginning to manifest itself in additional ways as well. We are noticing higher turnover rates. We find in some instances a declining quality of work and even actual sabotage. Neil Q. Hedrick, a labor department official and coauthor of *Where Have All the Robots Gone?*, has stated, "We cannot ignore the fact that young workers, even more than the oldest ones, want more out of a job than just a secure way to do an assignment, more than enough income to get a nice car and home. A good job to them, to be sure, has to be one with decent wages and job security, but those conditions no longer are enough to make and keep them satisfied with work or with their employer or with the union."

Some industrial engineers believe that American industry has in many instances pushed technology too far by taking the skill out of jobs; a point of human resistance has been reached. As one steel worker put it, "It is hard to take pride when you work for a large steel company. It is hard to take pride in the fact that you may never cross the bridge you help to build." Employees involved in mass production do not always see the end product of their labor. It is very difficult to inspire and instill pride in these people.

Another expression of dissatisfaction with work is what is known as the "job blahs" or the "Who wants to work?" syndrome. This solemn refrain is heard across the country by auto workers, aerospace technicians, people working as machine shop operators, or in some instances, senior management representatives. These men and women are the next problem children of the American economy. They are alienated workers afflicted with the "blue collar blues," the "white collar woes," and the plain "on-the-job blahs." They are bored, rebellious, and frustrated. Sometimes they are drunk on the job or "spaced out" on drugs. Sociologists and industrial psychologists are deeply interested in this group of people who are still largely a mystery to many of the people who should understand them best: their employers and their union leaders.

Sixty two percent of the country's 83 million workers are engaged in manufacturing. About one million of these are tied to the dull routine and tedium of an assembly line. The mood of this vast work force is obviously of tremendous importance to the country as a whole, as well as to the individuals themselves. Workers' attitudes clearly affect productivity and ultimately the standard of living.

In Japan, the typical manager takes a socially active part in all the affairs of the people that work for him, no matter what the level of the employee. This is an important part of Japanese society, but it is even more important because it enables a manager to become acquainted with his employees. They learn to understand each other, and an essential rapport develops. A nation's attitude toward work is extremely significant. This involves not only jobs, but a way of life for us in the United States.

While people have always complained about work, there is a widespread feeling that there is something different about today's discontent. As a result, the managers of American business and industry are now coming up with plan after plan to help pacify unhappy workers.

Even under ideal conditions, a certain amount of absenteeism is inevitable. For any company which has a product line type of activity, absenteeism is particularly important because it carries a very high price tag if not controlled. It has a very definite impact on product quality, on production schedules, and most important, on profit. That is generally where the managers and stockholders become interested.

Management can play an extremely important role in controlling absenteeism. This can best be done by centering attention on two major factors. First of all, no matter what kind of a job a person may have, the way he is treated has a direct bearing on his attendance record. Second, absence for both plant and office personnel is directly related to supervision, work associates, job status, job satisfaction, job interest, and job environment. These are important factors of which we have recently become aware.

Controlling absenteeism requires that the problem be handled at the lowest level of management, the foreman or supervisor. Here the worker must clearly understand the importance of his effort to the total team. When a worker is absent and his attendance record begins to look questionable, the supervisor must discover the reasons. He must check the frequencies of an employee's absences, find out how he is getting along, and talk to him when he returns to the job. On the basis of facts, the supervisor must evaluate the problem and decide what action should be taken. It is not enough for a supervisor to know that a worker will not be in on a certain day. He should try to distinguish between a good reason and a real reason for the absence.

In checking over a man's attendance record, more is involved than just knowing the days he has been off the job. There is a big difference between the worker who has been away from work for twenty days because of a gall bladder operation and a man who stayed home for one or two days on ten different occasions. Unless a supervisor keeps and understands absentee records, he cannot do a good job when trying to get to the root of the problem.

Through keeping records, it is possible to identify patterns and attempt to correct them. If an individual is away from work on an extended absence, a supervisor has a responsibility to call occasionally and find out how he is doing. It is essential that the worker know that he is missed on the job and to see whether he is getting proper medical care and attention. Contact of this kind is important both to cement relationships between the employer, the supervisor, and the individual employee and to help cut down preventable absenteeism.

It is possible that there would be fewer employees coming down with colds on the first day of the fishing season if the supervisor were conscientious in following through during the absence periods. When a worker returns to the job, some acknowledgment of the absence should be made, even if it consists only of asking him how he is feeling. If the employee was seriously ill, the supervisor should be certain that he has the job under control again, that he has been to the medical department and been granted proper release to return to his particular job.

In cases where it seems as though the absence was avoidable, where a man's record shows a high rate of absenteeism, where his excuses seem questionable, or where he is evasive about the reason for his being absent, an interview should be required to get to the root of the problem. It is necessary to discover exactly why the individual was away from the job and whether there were any hidden reasons for the absence. It is important to show the employee his record and to stress the importance of attendance. The supervisor should try to ascertain whether the situation that caused the absence has been brought under control.

The supervisor's attitude during this kind of interview should be one that will enable him to get the facts; he should be neither antagonistic nor excessively sympathetic. The matter should be treated constructively as a mutual problem.

What is learned during the interview determines the kind of action that the supervisor should take. It may mean referring the worker to outside help or counsel for a family problem, sending him for a medical check-up, or changing his job assignment. If it is clearly a disciplinary problem, the worker should be warned, and further unexcused absence may be reason for termination. It is not possible to maintain a professional team unless there is discipline among the employees.

One of the most valuable things any industrial executive can learn is the importance of being people-conscious. Dr. Mortimer Feinberg addresses this topic in his book, *Effective Psychology for Managers*. "To be effective as a manager of people you must first become sensitive to their image of you and second, you must be sensitive to their needs as individuals. Finally, you yourself must be capable of change." Your subordinates may require it. It was originally assumed that a supervisor had an either or choice, that he had to be either employee-oriented or production-oriented. As a supervisor became more employee-oriented, more compassionate and interested in his workers, he became less production-oriented, less mindful of production, quotas, and quality control. The reverse situation is also thought to be true. Studies at Ohio State University have shown that both employee and production-orientation can be woven together to produce more effective supervision. Most successful supervisors combine employee-centered and production-centered orientations, working out their own creative ways of synthesizing these two concerns.

Another extremely important factor in stable management-employee relationships is the leadership and the motivation that is generated by all levels of management. In this regard, I personally decided myself to the needs of my people by directly participating in all activities in order to better communicate and understand the working pulse of the facility. This includes getting to know the employees by meeting with them as frequently as possible. In a large organization, this means touring a different part of the factory each morning and learning who belongs where and what problems are bothering employees. In addition, occasional visits to the night shift can be productive. Organized sports competition and company picnics are good morale builders, as well as solidifiers of labor-management relations.

The importance of an explicit attendance policy cannot be overestimated. Control of absenteeism depends on employees knowing what is expected and what they must strive for. The employee must maintain acceptable health standards and take precautions against illness. Minor indispositions or inconveniences should not be permitted to keep an individual away from the job. Every effort should be made to live, work and operate safely, to observe safety rules and practices both on and off the job. Attendance to personal affairs and obligations is the employee's responsibilty, but if an individual has a real problem and needs some time off during the day, it can be worked out; he should not be fearful of requesting a special favor. All employees are expected to come to work regularly and on time. An extremely effective maneuver consists of the manager standing outside the plant, greeting every employee and glancing at his watch from time to time.

Equally important as the worker's responsibility to stay on the job is the manager's obligation to make sure that all employees and supervisors understand this policy. Adequate records are a must for any manager or executive who wants to understand how to work with people.

It is my conviction that absenteeism at any industrial facility is directly related to the industrial executive's involvement with that problem. Each employee is individually concerned about the future and his own self, and everyone must feel that management, too, is concerned about his as an individual. I have never seen a successful supervisor or executive, a man who could motivate the people beneath him, who was not himself highly motivated. The best motivators of people are those who themselves are hardworking, almost to the point of total commitment to their work. You motivate by example, and the degree of your motivation will reflect directly on the quality of performance of your employees.

Absenteeism represents a growing national problem in industry. It can be curbed, however, if management will recognize the importance of becoming totally involved in the human relations problems of people, particularly as they relate to job performance, production, working conditions, motivation, and effective communication. The importance of industrial psychology and working directly with employees cannot be overemphasized.

DISCUSSION

Panelists in this discussion included Harold A. Abramson, M.D., Director of Research, South Oaks Foundation; Orman Crocker, Executive Director for the Long Island Council on Alcoholism; and J. L. Kaull, Manager, Manpower Development for the Hazeltine Corporation. Others were Eileen D. McDermott, Assistant Vice President, National Bank of North America; Robert S. Millen, M.D., Medical Director for the New York Stock Exchange; and Granville I. Walker, M.D., Medical Director for the Chase Manhattan Bank.

Mr. Crocker:

As Executive Director of the Long Island Council on Alcoholism, this is my main concern. Alcoholism is a very serious problem which results in continuing and progressively worse absenteeism. The Council serves as a referral source for employee who exhibit symptoms of alcoholism.

Ms. McDermott:

I handle employee relations problems in a bank. I have found that absenteeism can be symptomatic of an employee problem which comes to light when the individual is referred to the personnel department. Employees are often reluctant to speak to their supervisors about personal problems, and consequently their problems are rarely dealt with until they reach a very serious stage. I am interested in finding ways to deal with empolyees' problems before they are serious that absenteeism becomes a basic symptom.

Dr. Abramson:

I am concerned with psychoanalytic theory as it pertains to management. To understand absenteeism, we must understand the feelings of the white collar worker and the blue collar worker when one or the other is absent.

Dr. Millen:

I ran a private clinic which was set up to serve the New York Stock Exchange and its affiliated companies. The clinic was set up privately and functions with more doctors at less cost to the Exchange and with more specialities than a company-affiliated medical department could. In addition, we feel that we have better relationship with patients because of our private nature.

Dr. Walker:

I have found that most people have very little conception of what a bank physician does. There are thirty-three people who work in my medical department serving 25,000 employees. Six of these are physicians. In addition to seeing approximately 200 people with various problems per day, I try to have an impact on management and labor in terms of educating them as to the kinds of problems I see. I am convinced that if we are to have any long-term impact on absenteeism (as well as other human relations problems) we must deal with the environment, not only in the bank but also in the home and throughout the country.

Mr. Kaull:

I am concerned with the development of team work in our organizational structure and with the development of abilities for doing whatever has to be done at any level in the organization. If there is any area in which I spend a larger proportion of my time, it is in the field of management and executive development, management being interpreted from the lowest to the highest level of supervisory structure. I am concerned about both the performance of managers and their relationships to the rest of their particular organizations.

Question:

One of the problems in interviewing a person to determine the reason for absenteeism is that one may have to jump over the immediate supervisor. How can this be handled?

Ms. McDermott:

These are the steps my organization takes in dealing with absenteeism. First of all, we determine through our medical department whether the individual's medical history can account for recurring absences. If not, then the absenteeism has something other than a medical basis.

Next, we talk with the supervisor and obtain his permission and cooperation in having the individual come to the personnel department. We do not jump over the supervisor. Sometimes there is a certain amount of resistance on the part of the supervisor because if the employee is a chronic absentee problem, the supervisor is already angry about it. There is resentment on his part and on the part of the absentee's fellow workers. If there is insurmountable resistance from the supervisor, we generally get him to agree to a talk with personnel that might result in a transfer for the employee. If, after talking with the employee we feel that the absenteeism is correctable, there are two paths we can take. If the absenteeism is the result of indifference and the supervisor refuses to take the employee back, we may have to consider termination. If the employee is having family problems or other problems not in his control, we try to get him into counselling. If the employee is unable to return to his original supervisor, we must try to "sell" the individual to a new supervisor. We inform the new supervisor of the absentee problem and assure him that we are taking steps to correct the problem.

Dr. Millen:

The New York Medical Society had an industrial meeting recently. It was suggested there that when there is a great deal of absenteeism within one department, the personnel department would be wise to deal with the supervisor in addition to the individual employees.

Question:

Discretionary absences have been defined as those absences in which the individual could go to work. What percentage of absences are discretionary?

Audience:

I would suspect that a minimum of 30 percent of absenteeism is discretionary in the sense that the individual could, if he wanted to, come to work. I feel that the more comfortable, productive, and useful the work environment is made, the more people will use their descretion and decide to come to work rather than stay home.

Mr. Kaull:

Recently, a study was completed which focused on the relationship between the supervisor's behavior and absenteeism in his subordinates. The study indicated that there is a direct relationship between the way the supervisor conducts himself when subordinates have made mistakes and the attendance records of these subordinates.

For instance, when an employee has done a poor job and knows that his supervisor is extremely vociferous about his displeasure, he will tend to be absent on the day of or immediately after a performance appraisal.

We must try to create an environment in which the employee

does not dread coming to work. Supervisors and executives must take a positive approach.

Dr. Walker:

To a certain extent, the way an organization is run determines the kind of people who will work there. Only people who can adjust to the administration of a company will remain in that company's employ.

Dr. Millen:

It sometimes becomes very difficult to preach against discretionary absenteeism to the lower levels of employees. Too often, someone from upper management claims he has a cold when he wants to take a long weekend.

Question:

Do you have any ideas about differential absenteeism rates and reasons for absenteeism for blue collar versus white collar workers? In what ways can we deal effectively with different kinds of people?

Dr. Walker:

People will come to work in places where they enjoy working, feel productive, and feel respected as individuals. Certainly, creative people do better in this sort of environment. On the other hand, there are people who do very well in strange environments with highly authoritarian supervisors. It is very difficult to make general statements.

Mr. Kaull:

I agree with that. For instance, one of our plants employs almost exclusively blue collar workers, and the absenteeism there appeared to be getting out of hand at one point. The initial reaction to this situation was that the employees we had been hiring recently were of a lesser quality. This was certainly not supported by fact. We found, for example, that the absenteeism was greater for our older employees.

One of the things we found which contributed to absenteeism in this situation was that we had gone too far to the extreme in simplifying operations. We had made some of them too repetitive under the assumption that we would get more production. Instead, the element of boredom had entered the picture to such an extent that the people simply did not care about coming to work.

Another factor we found contributing to absenteeism was the fact that we were planning some consolidation and reorganization. A number of the people who were absent feared the loss of job or status to the extent that they were out looking for new jobs. In fact, we had no plans to terminate them. By finding out the real causes rather than dealing with generalities we were better able to deal with the situation.

Another example of the danger of reacting to generalities might be seen in a case of white collar absenteeism. In this situation, it was felt that a group of research engineers had been absent to excess. After exploring the situation further, it was found that the research projects for which they were responsible were proceeding far ahead of schedule. The researchers had been working around the clock, and they were now catching up on some much needed rest. It was decided that the important thing was not the hours of the day these individuals were on the job, but what they accomplished. Absenteeism problems must be viewed from different perspective depending on the circumstances, not handled by an inflexible policy or procedure.

Question:

At South Oaks Hospital, we have a geriatric unit. When some of our employees are assigned there, they are often absent, and we realize that this is because of their dislike of the work. We have tried to motivate them in different ways, but have found that these individuals simply find different ways of avoiding the work. How can this be handled?

Audience:

Perhaps the problem could be eliminated by rewarding those who work in the geriatric unit.

Dr. Walker:

I am not sure that a reward would solve the problem. In the final analysis, you must find people who have a positive motivation toward working with older people based on their own inner chemistry.

Question:

How does industry deal with and react to individuals who abuse drugs?

Dr. Millen:

If we find an employee who admits to using drugs we encourage him to resign so that he will not be terminated and branded as a drug user. He is also encouraged to obtain treatment. We do urinalysis to detect drugs on every individual who reapplies for employment.

Mr. Kaull:

As a company, we knowingly have hired a limited number of people who have been on drugs and who have been rehabilitated or are in the process of rehabilitation.

Occasionally, we find an employee using drugs when we were not aware of his or her problem. They are not automatically terminated. In each case, we have to ask ourselves several questions before dealing with the individual. First of all, we must ascertain whether the individual works in a government department with a defense type of project line or whether he works in a department where security is not a problem .

Next, we determine the individual's contribution to the company and to himself, whether he is progressing, and whether we can help him. We must study each case individually. Finally, there is the factor of the corporate commitment to this kind of social problem. Then we decide how far we want to go in contributing to the solution of each problem.

Question:

Has there been any progress in getting people to accept alcoholism as a serious disease?

Mr. Crocker:

I find in my work that in most corporations upper echelon management is very reluctant to consider the problem of alcoholism in their particular environment. There are very few dynamic and productive industrial alcoholism programs in existence. The major health problem in industry today is alcoholism. Yet most of the corporate programs involving treatment of alcoholism or dealing with the alcoholic problem in the plant die before they are developed because of resistance at the upper level. In fact, many upper management people are naive enough to claim that they "don't hire that kind of person."

The following is a statement from the National Council on Alcoholism:

> In one year I have come to realize that the denial syndromes surrounding corporation can be thicker than the one surrounding the alcoholic. Management can and does act as co-alcoholic with the employees, especially long-time or executive employees. They will fire new people but go into horrors about calling a family member that nasty old word, "alcoholic." They say the "family member" or executive may be sick indeed and may drink all the time but certainly he is no alcoholic. They may be problem drinkers, but they are not alcoholics. Non-alcoholic alcoholics, a product of corporate denial.

Mr. Kaull:

A first line supervisor who does not consider alcoholism in his subordinates a problem that should be recognized feels he is doing the individual a service by concealing the alcohol abuse. By giving the alcoholic compassion instead of help, he can easily compound the drinker's problem. Too many people consider alcoholism a social disgrace and not a disease.

Mr. Crocker:

I often wonder who supervises the supervisors. I would venture to say that as many as 10 percent of first line supervisors are alcoholics themselves.

Audience:

Alcoholics are absentees in a very special way, in addition to the Mondays and Fridays they take off. It is not the total day or week off, but the accumulated latenesses which affect production. The long lunch hour, extended trips to the rest room, and appointments to see counselors about the problem all add up to decrease productivity.

All organizations should seriously consider helping the alcoholic employee to obtain treatment. In terms of economics, it is much cheaper to pay a man his salary for one month while he is being treated for alcoholism than to have to pay the compensation that would be necessary if he had a serious accident on the job because of his alcoholic condition.

Question:

It seems fashionable right now for companies to be committed to the concepts of job enrichment, job enlargement, and motivation, as well as to employ behavioral scientists and industrial psychologists to reduce discretionary absenteeism. To what extent is this commitment real?

Mr. Kaull:

I think it is a matter of practicality rather than idealism. I mentioned before that a factor contributing to absenteeism is boredom. The only thing to do is to remove the boredom, and in my opinion, expanding the scope of operation is the answer. I do not believe that companies are taking an idealistic position by considering job enrichment and the value of using industrial psychologists. They are simply recognizing the fact that it is necessary to motivate people by positive action.

It is generally agreed that if we can motivate people to come to work, we will not have to worry about absenteeism. It has generally been thought that money is a prime motivator. When pay is used as an incentive merit increases are often treated as rewards for coming to work for the required period of time. It is found that this idea does not really work all that well. Consequently, industry is beginning to look for different ways of motivating people.

Question:

Why is alcoholism in upper management often overlooked?

Dr. Abramson:

In my experience, management provides thinking rather than product. Many upper managers or researchers are unique in that they are knowledgeable in a certain area. They become indispensable to the companies that employ them. We cannot monitor or criticize these professionals so long as their thinking is acceptable. The real professional turns out ideas rather than products.

It is not so much that professionals' problems are overlooked or ignored as they are accepted because of these individuals' value to the organization. There is a qualitative difference between the white collar and blue collar worker.

Question:

But isn't threat of job loss the most effective motivation?

Mr. Kaull:

Threat of job loss, while sometimes an effective device, is very much oversold. I would suggest that it be used only as a last resort and that more energy be devoted to find positive ways of influencing people. We sometimes see this threat applied frequently and readily to blue collar workers but not so quickly to professional employees. It may be that the difference between the very necessary professional person and the blue collar worker is that we exert greater effort and try more ways to get these individuals to get help for their problems. It often seems that we are more tolerant of problems with the professional. Actually, we simply spend more time trying to positively influence them than we would with someone regarded as less essential to the success of the organization. I am not sure that this is the right approach to take. Everyone is entitled to equal treatment.

Dr. Abramson:

One of the most interesting things I have found in my private practice is the correlation between problems at work and problems at home. Home problems are usually relatively easy to deal with, and when they are solved, work efficiently accordingly.

Mr. Crocker:

In the field of alcoholism, it is generally accepted that the point at which the alcoholism endangers the professional's job comes about seven years after the appearance of problems in the home. If management could look into the home environment of each of their employees, many of these initial problems would be eliminated or picked up long before they surface and cause a complete collapse in the individual. This is the real function of intervention. If we had the opportunity to view these initial problems in advance of the final collapse, much absenteeism could be eliminated and perhaps many lives could be saved.

Dr. Walker:

If absenteeism or any other problem is to be solved we must use a highly multidisciplinary approach. We cannot look for a perfect solution from any single area.

Chapter 3

THE PERSONNEL DIRECTOR LOOKS AT ABSENTEEISM

Daniel Knowles*

C ONTRARY TO POPULAR ROMANTIC OPINION, absence, at least in the eyes of personnel director, does not make the heart grow fonder. In fact, theory suggests that absenteeism is merely a fore-runner of turnover, and today's absentee is tomorrow's quit or discharge. Certainly no company wants a large turnover in its staff. The obvious cost to a company which requires a continuous stream of new employees is tremendous. Given the merits of such a theory, it is incumbent then upon a personnel director to examine this galloping precursor of turnover and head it off at the pass.

In too many organizations preventive actions are limited to flu shots, while personnel and organizational problems have actions taken only in response to crisis. The result is that precious time is consumed putting out the day to day brush fires.

Absenteeism is a real and present danger to corporate profits and effectiveness, and it must be attacked with a positive program to reduce it. As in any such program, we must first identify the problem and define it. The danger in definition, of course, is apparent from the parable of the Blind Men and the Elephant: Each blind man coming upon the elephant felt a different part

---

*Daniel Knowles has been involved in personnel work for many years. Currently the Director of Personnel for Grumman Aerospace Corporation, he has held similar positions with Fairchild Hiller and with a subsidiary of American Airlines. He has also served as Assistant to the Vice-President for Industrial Relations at Sperry Gyroscope Corporation. In addition, Mr. Knowles has been President of the Long Island Personnel Directors Association and serves on the faculties of a number of universities in the New York Metropolitan area.

of the animal and so described it differently. Analogously, it is obvious that a definition of the problem at hand does not necessarily imply that we understand it.

In the past absenteeism has been defined variously as absence from work (the most simple definition) to absence for which no satisfactory excuse is given, to all absences beyond a certain number of days. All such definitions have one common denominator. They treat absenteeism as the common cold, an affliction common to all. Absentees cannot, however, be grouped by sheer statistical numbers. One cannot group them as a whole and expect to fully understand and then treat the problem.

Absenteeism is an individual problem and can take many forms, ranging from the newly-hired employee who never shows up for work, to the employee who takes long weekends, to the ten-year employee coming to work five or ten minutes late each morning. Once management had convinced itself that absenteeism was costly, it tried to convince the employee. Over the years this has brought about literally dozens of techniques for reducing absenteeism such as sending letters to the employee, putting posters on bulletin boards, and giving various warnings, reprimands, and disciplinary measures to the employee.

These approaches to the individual employee gave rise to a program which allegedly is effective in combatting absenteeism in some companies: On the first and second unexcused absences one gives warnings; on the third the employee is terminated. Apparently it is effective because not one employee has ever taken more than three unexcused absences! Interestingly, but not surprisingly, while the absentee rate was reduced, the turnover rate remained constant. What all this comes down to is that too many concerns are treating the symptoms and not the cause.

There are many reasons individuals give for taking time off from work. Many of these absences, viewed superficially, appear to be unavoidable but are in fact often avoidable. The personnel manager who recognizes the dire effects of a high absentee rate should also recognize the need and value of long term, ongoing programs to combat absenteeism and reduce the legitimate but avoidable absences.

Sickness is probably the one major reason people give for absence. It is amazing how many people profess to be in good health but who call in giving reasons for absence which are symptomatic of overall poor physical condition. Nevertheless, aside from such excuses, there is a statistical segment of the employee population which does get ill as is evident from the records of employees who are absent three or more days in succession. Ongoing health programs can offer such preventive measures as free influenza shots, cancer detection information meetings, periodic physicals for certain management levels, and making available complete medical checkups for all employees when they reach a certain age. Such programs can definitely reduce time lost from work by preventing serious illness, which often is not only more costly in terms of some form of extended pay with zero productivity but is emotionally debilitating to the employee.

These preventive health programs are invaluable as an aid to the morale of the staff and to their personal emotional well-being. Closely related to this is the mental and emotional health of employees. Counselling services, when adequate, can provide direction and guidance to employees who otherwise may suffer emotional frustration and anguish which seriously hamper their effectiveness at work.

A most serious problem is the recognition of alcoholism. Effective programs dealing with the alcoholic as well as the drug abuser should be in operation to avoid the loss of valuable personnel to an organization.

If the emphasis on equal opportunity over the past decade has taught us anything, it has given us an appreciation of the fact that we are all, in the final analysis, a minority of one. Blue collar and white collar distinctions have lost some of their impact. We are aware of the problems of the older worker, the female worker, the ethnic minority, and so on. This will be the realization of the 1970's in the business world: the individualization of the employee. Each employee has an age, sex, ethnic background, and experience which make him unique. The importance of the individual self must be recognized by the business community, or the individual will increasingly be alienated by it.

More and more positive actions are being taken to provide a more individualized environment at work and thereby an enhancement of the self-worth of the individual. In my company, for example, we tried to innovate by discarding time cards for clocking out at the end of a work shift. We now provide more opportunity for individual decision making on the job by a reduction in supervision from a ratio of one supervisor for each six employees to one supervisor for each eighteen employees. We have made provisions to allow employees time away from the job to attend to personal business. This recognizes an employee's personal life to have reasonable priority over the work environment as opposed to the traditional time off only when sick. Elsewhere, we are watching the effect of the institution of flexible working hours which enable the employees to vary their starting and quitting times as suits their personal needs.

Additionally, then, we must now realize that absenteeism is not simply a problem seeking a solution, but it is a social indicator which reflects the times. While some of the traditional reasons that cause people to stay away from work still remain, others have arisen. While it is impractical at present to effectively or economically treat each employee as an absolute individual, we must recognize the significance of factors which make the individual part of a special group. On a larger scale, we must recognize that there are factors which affect all employees and to which all companies will hopefully address themselves.

The past theories about security and wages are not as important any longer, although they are still present and significant in some cases. Two new factors must be considered if we are to effectively analyze absenteeism as a symptom of a discontented employee. We are continually advancing into a world of leisure, and we are becoming an ever more educated society. These two factors greatly contribute to the dynamics of absenteeism analysis.

Let us consider for the moment the impact of leisure. Traditionally, the two days of the week that are most affected by employee absenteeism are Monday and Friday. The reasoning for this, by and large, has been to obtain a longer weekend. In 1970, the Federal government enacted legislation to change traditional holidays, such as Washington's Birthday, so that they are observed on Mondays, thereby providing more three-day weekends for workers. While some complain that it is even harder to come back to work after a long weekend, the facts are that most people do return, at least for now. Probably the most popular movement from the view of employees has been the move towards a four-day work week. Firms that have started such a work schedule report a dramatic reduction in absenteeism. The beauty of this plan is that it allows an employee a day off without penalizing his pay status or his work record.

We must not, however, delude ourselves with the thought that absenteeism is a desire solely for more leisure time. It is a desire in most cases to get away from the job. We are a more educated society with more awareness of the social world in which we live. This awareness has provided two generations of workers who are very aware of individual rights. They feel that it is incumbent upon the work environment to provide in exchange for their services not merely wages but security in the form of comfortable retirement and health benefits. Above all, employees desire a satisfactory and pleasing work place with an atmosphere free of psychological stresses and a job which is meaningful to the skills and ego of the individual. In addition, the employer is expected to care.

Anthropomorphic considerations aside, we refer to the parent company because the company is just that to its employees: a parent substitute. Employees consciously or unconsciously look at the company in that manner, and it is the wise company which provides an adequate response. As individual parents we nurture our children, educate them, and in short, provide everything we can for their adult success. The employer-employee relationship is somewhat similar. I do not mean to imply that a corporation should treat its employees like children. What I am saying is that a good family relationship in the home can be a model of sorts for a similar relationship at work.

Children run away from home when they cannot tolerate the family relationship. Employees become absentees when they run away from the work environment. Just as the needs of a child vary as he matures, so do the needs of workers vary depending on their sex, age, and marital status. I stress the individual needs of the employee because the reality of the situation is that regardless of whether one agrees or disagrees that a company should provide day care services, portal to portal transportation, psychological counseling, or any other such services, the employee who does not come to work is hurting the company, himself, and society. Often such services to the employee need not actually be provided by the company but should be available by utilizing outside sources and agencies. The company that takes the time to make such referrals shows its concern, and the employee will not run away from such an employer.

Of course I am aware that to deal with each employee as an individual is a quantum jump in industrial relations as it is commonly practiced and may well be impractical. Nevertheless, it is necessary to deal with something substantially less than the corporate population to be effective in a program to reduce absenteeism. There really is not one all encompassing panacea. On the grand scale, we must offer redesigned work positions and job duties to offer meaningful work to independent, well-educated, thinking individuals. Work must not be a mind-numbing routine, a hair's breadth away from automation. We must also offer a program which enables the employees to feel a sense of security beyond his weekly paycheck.

Next, we must sort out the groups of employees with particular needs—minority ethnic groups, older workers, and women workers. Addressing ourselves to the needs of these significant groups will be rewarding in terms of cooperative responses obtained from the employees. A word of caution is in order here. Companies must address themselves to the needs of as many of these groups as possible but should be wary of concentrating on only one group. Providing special attention to one group has with it all the dangers inherent in and the untoward aspects attendant to a policy of nepotism or favoritism. It may be rejected by the receiver and resented by the observers. These efforts, however, properly carried out, will reduce absenteeism and keep it down far more than disciplinary measures and threats of termination;

this is a program which will be receptive to the needs of the individual employee and will change with the times. Above all else, it is a program which is empathetic to the employee and which cares about him.

About 50 percent of the people who come to a personnel department to complain about some problem are usually coming in to complain about money. If the personnel director has the capacity, time, willingness, or interest to do an in-depth type of interview, it is interesting to find that at least half of these people are not complaining about money at all. Grown men are not supposed to come to the personnel department and say, "My problem is that my boss doesn't love me." Since a man is usually embarrassed to admit that he is unhappy with the lack of rapport he has with his supervisor, he goes through a process of rationalization and brings it down to something that is concrete, that is observable, that can be seen and understood by everyone. He draws the conclusion that, "If I have to work for that man, they are going to have to pay me another one thousand dollars a year." This is one of the two major reasons that people develop morale problems, become absentees, and end by quitting their jobs.

The other half of the people who are complaining about money generally are not complaining about the absolute dollars of their salaries, but rather the relativity of their salaries to their peers. Again, they are basically suggesting that they do not really feel that they are getting a fair shake from the people who are supervising.

The second major problem that I have observed in terms of causing morale problems, absenteeism, and quitting is the problem of underchallenging people, having them underemployed, not utilizing their talents to the maximum. As an example, hiring an engineer with the Ph.D. and having him do engineering aide work is underemploying him, as is hiring an electronic technician and asking him to test light bulbs.

Philosophically, the definition of happiness is the exercising of one's spiritual energies to the maximum. What this suggests is that if an individual does not have an environment in which he can exercise his talents and capabilities to the maximum, he will become and employee with a morale problem. It is not always the supervisor's fault; in some instances it can be the company's fault, e.g. during a period of retrenchment and when many people are going back to lower skilled jobs. It does not really matter what the cause is. If a person is working beneath his capabilities he is going to have a morale problem. Part of our hope lies in the area of trying to educate supervisors and managers in human relations.

Some of the experimentation that has been done in industry indicates that under the democratic approach to leadership, better group morale, group cohesiveness, and quality of product result. The only thing that is improved under the autocratic leader is level of production. However, the autocratic leader must never leave his work area, never turn his back on his employees, never become ill, never go to a meeting, never take a vacation day; as the autocratic leader leaves the work area, production goes straight downhill to a much greater extent than when the democratic leader leaves the work area. It is extremely difficult and perhaps impossible to change a supervisor in terms of his personality and his overview on life.

Consequently, the final hope is to convince supervisors and managers to change their *overt* behavior. They should do so through their intellect in dealing with any individual employee so that they will meet on the same grounds and in a manner that will encourage the employee to be as productive as he possibly can.

The reasons for chronic absenteeism are emotional, and emotions like love and hate are contagious. If a company cares for its employees, the employees will care for the company, and people who care about each other do not want to be apart.

DISCUSSION

Panelists in this discussion are all involved in personnel aspects of industry. They included Peter J. Andresakis, Employee Relations Manager, Doubleday and Company, Inc.; Ronald J. Edeen, Director of Probation for Suffolk County, New York; Mark E. Fox, M.D., Medical Director for the Long Island Railroad; and G. C. Kitts, Manager of Employee Benefits and Services for AIL, a division of Cutler-Hammer. Others were Daniel Knowles, Director of Personnel for Grumman Aerospace Corporation; Peter Krajeski, Director of Personnel for South Oaks Hospital, Amityville, New York; William J. Neenan, Personnel Counsellor for New York Life Insurance Company; and Frederick A. Whitehouse, Ed.D., Profesor of Education and Coordinator of Rehabilitation for the Counsellor Training Program at Hofstra University.

Question:

How has absenteeism come to be such a major industrial problem?

Dr. Snyder:

As human society has evolved through history, more and more elaborate systems for the organization of human activity have developed. The purpose of these systems has been to ensure the effective distribution of human energy and natural resources and thereby guarantee the continued protection of the species. In recent times, the industrial corporation has emerged as the predominant system for the organization of human economic activity. For countless generations, goods and services needed by society were provided for the most part by independent communities, guilds, or families of tradesmen and farmers. To work under this system of economic organization meant being rugged and perhaps ruthless, but above all, being in touch with other people.

Such a primitive system, however, proved inadequate to the task of providing the always increasing quantities of goods and services needed by populations that were expanding both numerically and geographically. Only the industrial organization with its capacity to swallow up capital and arrange production activity into separate distinct units was able to respond effectively to the needs of society as a whole. This system is necessarily vast and impersonal and has no commercially justifiable use for the human relationships so essential to the economy of the past. This often noted tendency of industrial organization to dehumanize work and the worker has always engendered considerable resistance. Today, this resistance is evident not only in the persistent complaints and threats of organized labor but in the spread of absenteeism to all levels of the industrial population.

Dr. Fox:

I am concerned about absenteeism from a moral point of view. Employees who are not at work often get into some kind of trouble, and I feel that this situation must be avoided. The devil finds work for idle hands.

I would like to make a definite distinction between absenteeism, which I feel is an industrial epithet, and illness. If an employee has the misfortune to be ill and is being treated for a very definite illness, I would by no means call this absenteeism. Absenteeism always implies a certain chronicity and repetivity, along with a certain degree of falsification. That is, the reason given does not always correspond to the real reason for the absence.

One very important factor in absenteeism is monetary gain. In the present structure of industry, there are people who have greater take-home pay when they are away from work for an alleged illness than when they work. In certain industries, the longer one stays away and the more one is able to impress someone else with the seriousness of disability, the greater the amount of money he will receive. This protracted, deliberate staying away from the job for monetary gain is an extremely important aspect of absenteeism.

Question:

When you have identified an employee as an abuser of time and attendance rules, what role do you see the personnel director playing? Is it primarily as disciplinarian or as counselor?

Mr. Andresakis:

This depends to a great extent on the company and the facilities and research available to it. The company should play an active role, and this role should not be identical in all cases for all employees.

I am speaking now of product absenteeism; the employee who could have been at work but was not. The absentee employee's immediate supervisor should be his first contact when he comes back to work. The individual's length of service and his value to the organization should determine the time spent in counselling him. The next step is for some member of the personnel staff to counsel on the importance of being on the job and to try to get at the underlying reasons for the absence. There should be a company policy regarding how many instances of absenteeism will result in termination. This is when the personnel staff becomes disciplinarian in nature. In some cases, particularly with young people, positive effects come from using the disciplinarian approach in the beginning.

Practically speaking, however, whenever job applicants are numerous, the company's tolerance for absenteeism goes down; when employees are hard to find, companies raise their tolerance limits.

Question:

What is the general policy regarding pregnant employees?

Mr. Knowles:

Traditionally, a company would set a general policy that all pregnant employees were required to stop work at the end of the sixth month of pregnancy. It is no longer easy to retain that sort of policy because not every woman needs to stop work at the same time. Today, most companies have made their policies more flexible by suggesting that pregnant employees stop working at the end of the second trimester of pregnancy. However, should a woman wish to stay beyond that period of time, she should submit a note from her personal physician to the medical department certifying that it is permissible that she remain in the active employ of the company.

Mr. Kitts:

In our company, we permit the pregnant employee to go on leave in accordance with the medical leave policy, that is to say, the leave starts when her physical condition prevents her from working. By the same token and again in accordance with the medical leave policy, when the individual is physically able to return to work, she must return. Six weeks after delivery is observed as the period within which the employee must return to work. If she does not return to work because she wants to care for the child, she is no longer considered a medical case but is viewed as having withdrawn voluntarily from the work force. We keep the employee's name on a waiting list and will give her preference in hiring when an opening occurs, if she so desires.

We have made the maternity leave policy coincide to the fullest extent possible with the medical leave policy, with the one exception that the pregnant employee does not receive disability pay. We base our decision not to pay disability benefits on the fact that the New York State Legislature had this under consideration in 1972 and did not act on it.

Dr. Fox:

It seems that the general policy in industry today is that a woman should remain at work as long as she feels physically and mentally able to continue on the job. The policy must be individualized to a person's occupation, tastes, and inclinations.

Question:

If, at the end of the six weeks after delivery, the employee should develop a complication because of that delivery, does she receive disability pay?

Mr. Kitts:

Our policy is that long-term disability insurance would not cover that sort of complication. The individual's medical insurance would still be in effect and would cover hospitalization, surgery, and doctor bills, but she would not receive any reimbursement in lieu of lost wages at that point.

Mr. Krajeski:

Since industry is continually revised by pressures from society, I would venture to say that disability pay will be applied to absences for reasons of pregnancy in a few short years.

Question:

What is the impact of all these corporation policies on the family constellation? What should the responsibility of industry be in its relationships with the family in our society?

Mr. Knowles:

Many of the functions of the family have been assumed by both government and the corporation in the past thirty years. The question relates very much to the question of paying subsidies to pregnant employees.

We must make a distinction between the kinds of reasons women may have for going to work in the first place. They may go to work at meaningful jobs to fulfill a potential as human beings or they may go to work simply because they need the money to support their families. If the former is the case, I really do not know what role the corporation can play in helping to take over some of the responsibilities of the wife and mother. However, the latter reason for going to work suggests that the corporation, in assuming certain responsibilities, should support a woman who is forced to leave work to take care of her family.

I do not think that the corporation and industry today know exactly what their role is in society. Historically, the corporation has been a profit-making organization at work in the market place, producing products, and selling them at a profit. Today, in light of the shrinkage of the individual's capacity to effect the decisions that manage his life, the corporation is being called upon to make socially beneficial decisions.

Question:

To my knowledge, there are only twelve major corporations in the United States that show an awareness of the problem of alcoholism to the extent that they are taking significant steps towards helping and intervening with alcoholics. Why is it that so many other companies have not taken steps to promote alcoholism intervention?

Mr. Neenan:

One of the deterrents to a good prognosis for alcoholism in this country is society's reluctance to accept alcoholism as a disease. In my own experience, the greatest problem is not motivating the alcoholic to stop drinking. It is motivating administrative managers and supervisors to refer problem drinkers to the medical department.

Question:

Do you feel that a good alcoholism program pays off financially?

Mr. Neenan:

Definitely. By rehabilitating employees, we do not have to train replacements. In addition, rehabilitated employees now perform at full capacity. Unfortunately, however, it is very difficult to convince a fifty-year-old manager to change his attitude toward problem drinking. It is much easier to sweep such problems under the rug.

Question:

Is absenteeism the only factor in the alcoholic profile?

Mr. Neenan:

No, it is one factor. In my own company, I ask the department managers to keep me posted on suspicious absenteeism, particularly when there is a pattern to the missed days. When I am notified of such a situation, I personally pay the employee a visit and determine the cause of the absenteeism. In most cases, it is alcohol abuse. I confront the employee and give him the choice of cooperating with the company recovery and rehabilitation program. By not cooperating, he runs the risk of final termination not because he is an alcoholic, but on the basis of his work performance as well as his attendance record.

Question:

In my own experience, I have found that many personnel directors resist the concept of alcoholism as a disease. They continue to consider the problem moralistically. How do you deal with alcoholism?

Mr. Knowles:

In my experience, most of the personnel people I know are reasonably enlightened in terms of alcoholism. The first step, from the personnel director's point of view, is a statement of policy on the part of the company. In my company we look at alcoholism as a medical problem before it becomes necessary to look at it as a personnel problem. The second step in dealing with alcoholism is the development of an industrial education program which takes place on many different levels, one of which is in the area of supervisory development programs. We do not want supervisors to play the role of diagnostician, but to keep their suspicions alive in terms of absenteeism and job performance.

An employee has every right to spend the weekend drinking, but when the problem reaches the point where it affects job performance, the company has a perfect right to take some action. In my company, we ask the supervisors to discuss their suspicions with their own bosses and then to contact the personnel department. A personnel relations representative discusses with the supervisor his suspicions. If it appears that there is a foundation for the suspicion, we set up an appointment for the employee with the medical department. Traditionally, alcoholics do not want to visit the company doctor. Supervisors are instructed to insist as a condition of continued employment that the employee present himself to the medical department.

If the medical department finds support for the possibility of alcoholism, the employee is referred to the National Council on Alcoholism. Treatment proceeds from there.

Question:

What is your opinion on a three or four day work week on an individual basis for retired persons or women with families to care for?

Mr. Edeen:

I am very much in favor of such a plan.

Mr. Knowles:

Such a program would be appropriate for women who cannot work eight hours a day or for retired workers. If there is a need on the part of the organization to establish a part-time work schedule, such a program would be ideal. Most companies, however, are guided primarily from a pragmatic standpoint.

Audience:

Since there is so much Monday and Friday absenteeism, such a program might be used very effectively in industry. Retired individuals and experienced women with families could be hired on a "substitute" basis to work on these high absentee days.

Audience:

The four-day work week is another way to combat absenteeism. My company has reduced absenteeism dramatically by instituting the four-day work week as an overall company policy.

Mr. Krajeski:

As a personnel director, I find myself concerned with absenteeism as an indicator of job dissatisfaction and how we can deal with that dissatisfaction from a supervisory standpoint. Recently, a research project was completed by General Electric. One group of employees was encouraged to participate in the daily decisions that affected their jobs rather than being handed orders as was the other group. Absenteeism was actually 66 percent lower in the group in which the supervisor encouraged participative input from their employees.

Today's workers are, in effect, more questioning, more demanding, and better prepared educationally. We must approach this type of worker with a new attitude, not with a unidirectional approach which orders employees about. Our orders must be tested first on an employee force for feedback before issuing directives. As proven at General Electric, participative supervision should decrease absenteeism since it allows employees to assist in those decisions which affect their jobs. The final result should be an increase in job commitment and a corresponding decrease in job dissatisfaction and absenteeism.

Mr. Edeen:

I have worked in county government for over twenty years. Recently, cost factors have become more important to us. Today, people in county government are production conscious, yet we still preserve a more paternalistic attitude toward employees than is found in private industry.

The probation department is concerned with saving people, and therefore, we are very much aware of the various facilities for helping people in the community. When our own employees have problems which may lead to absenteeism, we tend to work with them in the same way we would work with a criminal offender with similar problems: by using all the resources available to us.

Dr. Whitehouse:

One of the most important things any company can do is to afford a degree of individualization to employees. We speak of this as an idealistic goal, yet the more we try to understand each individual as a person with special needs and interests, the easier is will be to institute changes in terms of redesigning jobs to produce better employees.

Dr. Fox:

The greatest motivation that any individual can have is doing the sort of work he enjoys doing. Unfortunately, everyone cannot make his life's work coincide with his ideal dream, but most people are able to approximate their desires. People should obtain early training in whatever it is that they want to do, to the extent that this is possible. Individuals should not be pressured by society into thinking that they must get Ph.D.'s.

Mr. Andresakis:

One of the best things any company can do to reduce absenteeism is to engage in job enrichment. Unfortunately, job enrichment is expensive, since it often requires getting rid of assembly line techniques. Some companies find that economically it is easier to deal with excessive absenteeism than to enrich jobs.

Another suggestion is the "legalization" of absenteeism. For instance, if a company finds that many individuals are absent on the first day of the hunting season, it could make that day an optional company holiday. In addition, we could allow our employees so many days per year as personal time off.

Job enrichment means adding complications and challenge to a simple job, and that means changing the entrance requirements. We, in industry, are moving too quickly towards mechanization, computerization, and breakdown of skills to work on job enrichment effectively.

Mr. Knowles:

If I had to look for one hope for the future in terms of trying to reduce absenteeism, I would probably have to hope that we could do more in the area of training supervisors to give them a realization of how to meet the needs of employees. I would like supervisors to learn to deal with people with tact, and to allow employees the respect and dignity that they essentially want. Until such time as the majority of our first line supervisors understand the necessity of meeting the needs of people on an individual basis, I do not think that we will make that much progress in reducing absenteeism.

Mr. Andresakis:

Supervisors must learn to make employees feel needed, particularly when these employees have been absent.

In addition, rather than using so much energy in exploring the problems of young employees, I think we should take some affirmative action in considering the needs and problems of our older employees. Middle-aged and older workers are often discriminated against in many insidious, covert ways (leading to absenteeism), and it is to this, too, that we should address ourselves in the future.

Dr. Snyder:

Perhaps an entirely different approach by industry is called for. Of course it would be greatly impractical for industry to imitate the form of the old system of economic organization by pretending to be a family for the worker. However, industry might try to recapture some of the spirit of the original system by finding some way for the employee to experience dignity, self-confidence, and pride in his work.

This would involve a structural overhaul of organizational techniques. One possibility might be the discarding of industrial divisions within a company and the formation of small but complete subcompanies. Each subcompany would be responsible for the total production of part of the industry's annual output and would compete with the other subcompanies. The people who work within each of these subcompanies would participate in the ownership and administration of the subcompany by recruiting their own employees, managing their own advertising campaigns, and sharing in those profits the subcompany contributes to those of the whole corporation.

There is no guarantee that this sort of organization would solve all of the problems faced by industry today. However, in the light of the losses industry suffers every year as a result of worker absenteeism, such a proposal is worthy of consideration.

Chapter 4

LABOR LOOKS AT ABSENTEEISM

John J. McManus*

— — — — — — — — — — — —

THE CREDENTIALS OF ORGANIZED LABOR were established decades ago. Today we are still fighting for many of the same objectives we started with which are related to the topic of absenteeism. We want more and better jobs at higher wages, decent housing, a health system that not only cares for our sicknesses and accidents, but also prevents illness. We continue to fight for civil rights, education, and prepaid legal service. If it has to do with social progress, labor is in the forefront.

At the core of all this are jobs and wages. We are not ashamed to say so, even if it makes us look like grubby materialists in the eyes of our critics. Some of our critics claim a monopoly on idealism. They are reportedly interested in the welfare of all people, whereas the labor movement is considered a narrow, special interest group that only cares about getting more money for one segment of the population. Supposedly, we do not respond to high ideals, but only to the greed of our members. In point of fact, better jobs and wages are the keystone of everything we need to make America better. Clearly, what good is education if there are not enough jobs to go around? All we will end up with is the most educated army of unemployed in the world. What good is civil rights legislation of a black man is trapped in a ghetto by poverty? What good is the social security program if a man cannot earn a decent living during his working years?

---

*John J. McManus, A.C.S.W., is Assistant Director for the Department of Community Services of the AFL/CIO. Prior to taking that position he was Executive Director of the United Fund of Long Island, New York, Nassau County Commissioner of Public Welfare, and Executive Director of the Health and Welfare Council of Nassau County, New York.

The unions may represent only one segment of society, our membership, but in a larger sense we represent the interests of all working people, of all wage and salary earners. This group makes up about three quarters of the entire population. They make up the bulk of the nation's consumers and provide the market for an expanding economy; their purchasing power comes mainly from wages and salaries, not from dividends, capital gains, interest rates for executive compensation, or from the benefits of an absentee industrial conglomerate.

Labor has come a long way since the beginning fight for a living wage, and today there is much more of a fight. Even now in 1973 we continue to fight for the principle that no man should live in poverty who works forty hours a week, fifty-two weeks a year. Organized labor has been interested in the subject of absenteeism from the beginnings of the labor movement. From the first use of a collective bargaining approach to labor-management negotiations, absenteeism has been involved. It probably was present in the beginnings of union organization of the railroads when management literally chained firemen to the cabs of the locomotives so that they could not jump should the cab catch on fire. One Labor candidate for President of the United States ran for office from an Atlanta prison cell as a result of the locomotive chains issue.

The AFL/CIO Department of Community Services is vitally interested in absenteeism, as are all sections of organized labor. In particular, the Community Services Department accepts the reduction of absenteeism as a desirable objective of plant and community cooperation in providing the services to alleviate human misery. We are not committed to alleviate absenteeism, per se, but to the implementation of the principle that the life of a union member in his or her family should be made as healthy and happy as possible. In order to provide a fair measure of happiness, we believe that in addition to a good, full-time job, adequate pay, and benefits, a community must also provide the network of effective services, public or voluntary, that will help each of us to better adapt and survive in a highly complex and sometimes irritatingly difficult society.

A major precipitating factor in industrial or any other kind of absenteeism is emotional health and a feeling of well-being. Productivity for business and industry may be a critically important by-product. To establish the reduction and elimination of absenteeism as a major objective would be misleading and neglectful of basic problems and concerns. When employees have problems, management has a responsibility to help solve them. It is encouraging to note that more companies and corporations are easing up on what we refer to as management rigidity and are accepting the obligations that good citizenship includes.

We in the labor movement are in general agreement that the company does have a direct ongoing responsibility to its own employees. The 1973 strike by the AFL/CIO Oil, Chemical, and Atomic Workers is indicative of union activity in forcing a corporation to be responsible and forthright in meeting its obligations to employees' health. This applies not only in the plant, but is enmeshed with the life and the being and fiber of the community.

But where do we begin working on this problem? There are far too many instances in which we pay more attention to machines than to men. Machines are less expendable. We attend to them because we want them to be productive. We grease and oil them; we care for them and repair them. We cherish them at times as we cherish no man. Could this be an expression of our gadget-oriented civilization or a reflection of our basic values? Machines do not have emotions. Men do and workers do. Workers have emotions because they are human beings with all the hopes and fears and problems which all human beings share. Only when men become scarce do we learn to pay attention to them.

We can move forward another step by learning the worth of man as man and not only as a means to an end. This is what we might call our protein power. In our organized society, the emotional health of the individual worker is interrelated with the emotional health of his group and vice versa. This applies to a worker in a plant. It is impossible to separate his problems as a whole man outside the plant from his problems inside the plant. One has a direct bearing on the other. It is not enough to say that a man brings his problems into the plant. It would be more accurate to say that he takes his problems into the plant and out of the plant; both types of problems intermingle and are one.

What are the fears that workers share with one another? These include loss of a job, loss of health, loss of youth, and loss of purpose and personal fulfillment. These basic fears and their related anxieties call not only for cures but for prevention. This is a challenge, not only to employer and employee, company and union, but also to government, medicine, and the community at large. Our major objective should be to bridge the gap between promise and performance. Management can help with absenteeism in two major ways: through collective bargaining and through encouragement of community participation.

The essence of a wholesome employer-employee relationship involves recognition, respect, and remuneration. In terms of recognition, one of the ways to a sound work relationship is the prevention of confusing the false goals. This calls for genuine recognition by companies of unions as an important and integral part of our industrial society. It calls also for recognition by unions of an expanding socially responsible and free economy as a bulwark of political democracy and human freedom.

In the realm of respect, management should recognize that the employee is not a machine and that he does have emotions. He is a human being with a great many personal problems that may not necessarily be related to his job at the plant but which are influenced by the attitudes of the company and the behavior of its supervisory personnel. Management should respect the rights of employees to be themselves and to belong to organizations of their own choosing. At the same time, unions and employees should respect the rights of the company and its management personnel to direct, supervise, and coordinate to produce useful products and extend its markets. What I am suggesting is mutual respect for each other's rights, obligations, and prerogatives.

While a worker's feeling of belonging is best expressed through his union membership, he must also feel that he belongs as a vital member of the production team, that he gives it all he has, and that he produces something which is worthwhile to society and of which he has pride. It is no longer easy to feel that sense of pride which a master craftsman once felt when he produced with his own skilled hands and imaginative mind a pair of shoes, a watch, a garment. The production line and automation have made the old master craftsman almost a prehistoric being. It is still possible, however, to show respect for a man with a particular skill as a member of a group working with machines. The finished product of his labor should be described not only as the brain-child of Company XYZ, but, more important, as the handiwork of both Company XYZ and its employees, who happen to be members of Local 123.

The third contributing factor to a sound labor-management relationship is remuneration. A worker should be compensated adequately for his labors. He must be secure in the knowledge that he will not be thrown into the scrap heap in time of sickness and old age, that he will be provided with year round employment and advancement. Materialism and security are not ugly words. There is no spirituality in poverty, insecurity, and fear. Material wealth and security are good as long as they serve mankind to achieve a higher purpose in life, a life of creativeness and beauty and oneness. Labor is entitled to a fair share of the wealth that labor helps create as a matter of right and as a matter of justice.

I know of no collective bargaining agreement which covers material discord, juvenile problems, housing, education, recreation, adequate medical and dental care, legal aid, family counseling, and all other matters of a personal nature with which the individual worker and his family are concerned. Worried families produce worried workers, and worried workers do not produce and are absent from the job. It would seem to me that it is management's responsibility to its employees and to the company to provide help to the employees for personal problems not necessarily within the immediate realm of wages, hours, and working conditions. Industrial medicine, nursing, and counseling are some of the answers.

If it is to meet the great human and industrial need, industrial medicine will have to eliminate the possible suspicion that it is used against union organization and for the benefit of company profits only. To be truly effective, industrial medicine must have only one loyalty, not a loyalty to the company and not a loyalty to the union, but a loyalty to the sick human being and to the professional standards of ethics in industrial medicine. It is conceivable that the best approach in organized plants is through union-management sponsored medicine and counseling. In addition, restructuring of work can only be accomplished through collective bargaining. It is a management responsibility, too, to join forces with others to help develop and pay for community facilities, adequate medical care, hospitalization, family counseling, child welfare, schools, better housing, and other social services which will be available to all citizens, including the company's employees and their families.

Industrial medicine can at best only detect, refer, and possibly follow through; it cannot provide long-term treatment when necessary. There are relatively few communities in this country that have scheduled community services at clinics, agencies, and other treatment centers according to a worker's available time. When facilities are available only from nine o'clock to five o'clock, Monday through Friday, a worker who needs help will be forced to lose clock time and wages.

Good citizenship of a plant in a community will help produce good community citizens and more productive workers. It is to the advantage of all for management to support both public and voluntary community improvement projects. Sound public and community relations may be by-products, but the utlimate end-product is sound people.

A wholesome employer-employee relationship, a good industrial medicine program, and better and more available community facilities will all contribute to the emotional health of the worker, to the emotional health of the employer, and to the problem of absenteeism. When man, be he worker or employer, is emotionally aware of his full worth as a man, of his secure place in industry and society generally, of the love and respect of his fellow men, he will tend to become a vital force for good. We can learn from the past and apply its experience and knowledge within our present framework, but in the long run, emotional health is a personal and very intimate thing and cannot be produced on the assembly line. It means our own reeducation and perhaps our own salvation. What is required is the joint application of our total knowledge.

DISCUSSION

Panelists in this discussion included representatives of labor and management, as well as experts in the fields of medicine and law. Anthony J. Costaldo is Director of Community Services for the Long Island Federation of Labor of the AFL/CIO, and Micheal O. Diamond in Coordinator of the Employees' Assistance Unit, New York City Department of Sanitation. Others included the Honorable Jack J. Cannavo, Judge of the Family Court in Suffolk County; Capt. Patrick F. Carone, M.D. of the Department of Psychiatry at the U.S. Army Hospital in Kentucky; Paul J. Donnelly, Jr., Esq., General Attorney for the Long Island Railroad. Sidney Lang, Esq: is Supervising Attorney for the New York State Mental Health Information Service, Second Judicial Department, and Dr. Walter Gerstle is Regional Medical Director, New York State Employee Health Service.

Mr. Lang:

Absenteeism is definitely not a new problem. References to absenteeism have been found in remnants of ancient Egypt. The early Egyptians did not consider absenteeism a large problem, but attributed it to one of three reasons. The missing person was actually ill, or he was involved in appeasing the gods, or the individual was merely lazy. In business, the problem has not changed radically in all these thousands of years. It is basically the same problem.

Mr. Diamond:

In my opinion, one of the most successful and constructive approaches to the crippling absenteeism problem is the industrial alcoholism program. This program, which has shown a high success rate, involves management and unions in a joint effort to help the troubled employee. The criterion for success is job performance, and it is the supervisors who play the most direct role in implementing the program.

Dr. Gerstle:

In my specialty of occupational medicine, I have worked for both government and private industry. I have very strong feelings about the role of the industrial physician; he must be totally independent. Although the physician is by necessity on management's payroll, he cannot and should not be used by management or the union to its own advantage. It is frequently very difficult to convince a referred employee that the physician is not the tool of either party, but an impartial individual concerned only with the employee's well-being.

There are several factors which may contribute to absenteeism which have not yet been mentioned. One of these is "moonlighting." Many employees have two jobs or run a private business in addition to their industrial jobs. If the second job becomes too demanding, absenteeism from the industrial position will result.

Other factors leading to absenteeism are improper placement and borderline physical and emotional health. Many individuals stay away from their jobs out of fear of their own incompetence. Related to this is fear of one's supervisor. It is imperative that supervisors be trained in communication skills.

Question:

Do you feel that management or labor asks the company physician to corroborate a preconceived diagnosis when they send an employee for a checkup?

Dr. Gerstle:

I do not agree completely with that idea. What I do believe, however, is that the company becomes very angry with an employee who is chronically absent. Rather than handle the problem administratively, management may sometimes dodge the problem by sending the employee to the medical department in hopes that the industrial physician will find nothing wrong with the employee. This gives management a simple and direct reason to terminate the individual.

Hon. Cannavo:

I feel we would be extremely naive if we attempted to attribute absenteeism in industry to a single factor. Of course there are factors such as drug abuse (including alcoholism), occupational accidents caused by defective machinery or sluggishness on the part of the worker, strikes, and sabotage. Permissiveness has also been alluded to as a reason for absenteeism.

I feel that many of today's employees have developed a work ethic that states, "I can do as I like." Many workers have no duties or responsibilities to anyone but themselves. I still feel that the most important factor contributing to absenteeism is the alienation of the worker caused by dissatisfaction with the job. The cause here lies not in the worker. I believe that he is the victim of the industrial system, that the fault lies with industry and labor unions.

Over the past few decades, there has been a tremendous technological growth in industry. There has been a great deal of automation on the assembly line. This, of course, has resulted in workers who are bored and dissatisfied with their jobs. They are uninspired and feel that they are not accomplishing anything worthwhile.

Traditionally, management has been primarily concerned with increasing productivity, while labor has been concerned with higher wages and fringe benefits. It is important now that management and labor realize that in some industries nothing can be done about unchallenging jobs. Whenever possible, however, labor and management should make a joint attempt to redesign jobs so that workers become involved in decision making. Employees should feel that they themselves had something to do with a finished product, that their skills and efforts went into the ultimate product. I believe that when this is done, there will be a substantial reduction in absenteeism.

Mr. Costaldo:

My experience has been as Director of Community Services. In that regard, I run classes to train counsellors and also head a union which has to negotiate contracts and meet the problem of absenteeism. There are many reasons for absenteeism, and I feel that management and labor must deal with the problem jointly.

There is a certain amount of inevitable absenteeism due to physical illness. That sort of absenteeism is legitimate. One of the biggest factors contributing to absenteeism is alcoholism. Management and labor organizations can often see alcoholism developing. If it is not dealt with immediately, it will eventually have to be dealt with in its extreme form.

Alcoholism is a major problem, particularly because of the constant efforts of the liquor industry to encourage consumption of its product. We in community services recognize that alcoholism is rapidly becoming a more serious problem, particularly when drug abuse in general compounds the problem.

The general attitude of the younger segment of the work force adds to the absenteeism problem. These employees are not concerned with making a great deal of money, and they do not want to work for the "establishment."

Service industries are developing more and more as automation becomes more dominant. There is less and less manpower needed, and many problems result from this situation. The responsibility for finding solutions rests with labor and management as well as with the government.

Absenteeism is one of these problems. In solving this problem, it is necessary for both management and labor representatives to talk with the individual to get to the root of the problem. The cause may rest in the family situation or with the individual alone.

When an individual is first interviewed for a job, the personnel department receives some idea of what kind of person it is dealing with. If the individual is employed because there is no one else available, and the job must be filled, there is a greater chance of problems coming up.

The motivation of the work force has been a source of concern lately. It has been said that the work force is overeducated. No one can be overeducated. Some education is not relevant to job orientation, particularly when there are not enough jobs available in a particular field. For instance, about three years ago there was an overabundance of engineers. Students were cautioned to avoid engineering training because so many plants were closing down. We are presently finding ourselves with a shortage of engineers. In our industrial system, there is a continuous scrapping of talent.

Labor and management can reduce absenteeism by addressing themselves to the problem and the causes. If alcoholism or drug abuse is involved, constructive therapy should begin as soon as the problem is identified. If the absenteeism is more a function of motivation and monotony, attention should shift to an analysis of the job.

Audience:

My experience has been with a public school district. It seems that whenever we sit down to talk with labor in terms of coping with an absentee problem and trying to solve it, labor makes excessive demands. Management is asked to employ more people, to supply greater fringe benefits, and in general to do things that cost us more and more money. This is often beyond our capabilities, and the result is that we never solve anything. For instance, we try to provide an incentive for stacking up sick leave in terms of retirement benefits, but when we reach this plateau, labor demands payment for the accumulated sick leave at the end of each year. In no way has any of this cut down our absentee rate. I cannot believe that this is labor's viewpoint across the board.

Mr. Costaldo:

That is not our viewpoint at all. Any benefit that is written into the contract has a reason. Abuse of the benefit is another story, and organized labor does not condone this abuse.

Mr. Donnelly:

The foundations for a certain amount of absenteeism are laid when an individual is hired. As soon as an individual starts work, he is told that he can take off so many days per year. This immediately orients the individual to think about trying to get a little more.

The absenteeism I am discussing is not that resulting from alcoholism or drug abuse. What I am talking about is the "I don't want to go to work tomorrow, I think I'll go to a ball game" type of absenteeism. I feel that this attitude is a little insidious cancer in itself. The way to combat it is to orient the people correctly in the first place and then get them interested in their jobs. The most important thing that can be done is talking to employees on an individual basis.

Audience:

I would like to mention something in connection with my work on employment of the handicapped. Several studies have indicated that disabled people doing the same kind of work as their non-disabled counterparts come out the same or slightly better on indices of safety and absenteeism.

Research on collective bargaining agreements in New York State has been undertaken with respect to handicapped worker provisions in union-management agreements. This research may show some relevance to the question of absenteeism among disabled people and the way labor and management have treated disabling conditions.

The last thing I would like to dwell on is the practice of requiring layman supervisors to call in employees who have certificates of disability from private physicians. Who is the layman to judge the validity of a medical report? How can the layman supervisor judge whether an employee is sick or disabled enough to be excused for so many days? Perhaps the family physician should not be the one to make that decision, but neither should the supervisor without any medical training interfere in that judgment.

Dr. Gerstle:

The length of time an employee will stay away from the job depends on several things. If an employee breaks his leg taking out the garbage, it is an off-duty accident. As soon as his leg heals, the doctor will certify that the individual can return to work. If the same accident occurred while the individual was on duty, we would be confronted with a workman's compensation case. The various benefits the employee can accrue by not going back to work are overwhelming.

The time that an employee stays home also depends on his work task. The employee who performs a physically strenuous job would stay out longer than a supervisor or office clerk.

Thirdly, there are fashions in medicine. At one time, a woman would stay in bed for ten days after giving birth. Today, most women are back to almost normal routines within two or three days.

Finally, the supervisor is often left with deciding when an employee should return to work because most companies do not have the money or do not wish to spend the money for an independent medical service to make these decisions. In addition, there are not enough doctors who are interested in the less glamorous field of occupational medicine.

Mr. Donnelly:

The railroad and shipping industries are probably the only industries in this country that have legislation on the books which permits the employees to sue. The employee in these industries does not receive workmen's compensation. His only alternative is to sue the company.

This began years ago in the federal government because the railroad corporations were abusing the laborers. They were taking advantage of them by paying poor wages. The men were being badly hurt because the railroad industry is a dangerous one, and the railroads were making settlements which gave the injured employees a mere pittance.

The government passed what is known as the Federal Employer's Liability Act. This gave the railroad worker the right to sue. At first, this was an excellent idea, but in the last forty years it has been abused by the railroad employees. It is true that a man may be hurt, sometimes very badly, and he is entitled to take a long time off. However, there are many employees who have some minor injury and will take off up to ten weeks, knowing full well that when they get into court they will be reimbursed.

We have a very serious problem in that regard. This is one of our biggest segments of absenteeism. The employees know that they are going to be paid eventually, because the law is so written that they cannot possibly lose their lawsuits.

Mr. Lang:

I would like to discuss and formulate a definition of what absenteeism actually is. This is a rather complex area. Are all absences, whether justified or unjustified, to be considered instances of absenteeism? There are people who are actually sick, and management prefers that those people not be on the job. Just because the individual is sick does not mean that he is guilty of absenteeism. Are we talking about any and all instances that someone is absent? Isn't there justification for some absences?

Mr. Costaldo:

There is necessarily much diversity in the definitions of absenteeism because of the wide variety of items included or excluded by employers in defining and treating the various aspects of the problem. Absenteeism may be defined as the failure of workers to report on the job when they are scheduled to work. This may include both authorized and unauthorized absences, but not all employers count absences in this way.

In general, absenteeism includes loss of time because of sickness, accidents, or personal reasons as well as any unauthorized time away from the job. Some organizations include vacation time, military leave, or other excused leaves of absence. Some do not consider absence of less than half a day while others count any absence, even if only for an hour.

Statistics show that employees fall into three groups with respect to attendance: rarely or never absent, occasionally absent, and frequently absent. The latter account for the largest percentage of the absences, and it is this group that must be analyzed to evaluate and causes and determine possible solutions. In other words, the only aspect we should deal with is the unauthorized absences.

Hon. Cannavo:

It would seem to me that illnesses remain a constant factor every year. I do not believe that there has been any dramatic change from year to year in reference to excused absences due to illness unless there was some disaster in a particular area; I do not believe that we have ever had such a situation in this country, so I think we could safely disregard illnesses and accidents as a part of absenteeism.

Audience:

What you have said is true. You were talking about the legitimate absenteeism with which I would agree wholeheartedly. However, I do not think that we are really addressing ourselves to that alone. I think it is the extension of legitimate absence that is the real problem.

When an illness causes the initial absence (which would legitimately be limited to 2 or 3 days), but the employee has accumulated some thirty to fifty days, the individual will be more prone to take ten or fifteen days for a minor illness. I feel that it is this problem to which we should address ourselves as well as to the so-called illegitimate excuse for absenteeism. The important point is that there are many causes of absenteeism which originate legitimately but which are extended and abused.

Audience:

I am in charge of a program for the state which employs numerous workers. I have found to my dismay that below the supervisory level (where thirteen days of sick leave per year are permitted) practically every employee has by the end of the year consumed every one of those thirteen days, particularly the young people.

The young woman who is twenty-two years old is not concerned with saving sick leave for the future. She hopes to get married and retire. She is not interested in accumulating sick leave. Even the middle-aged person, if he is not in a supervisory capacity, does not worry about any catastrophe in the future for which he may need forty or fifty days.

I think that there are terrible abuses, and I think that underlying it all is human nature. No matter what is done, we will not be able to change human beings. The object is to minimize unnecessary absence. The only way to do this is through complete communication and rapport between unions and management.

Capt. Carone:

I would like to raise the question as to whether or not both management and labor are to blame for being too paternalistic. I think it is part of human nature that when one is under an authority he tries to get as much as he can. The important question that comes up concerns who takes the responsibility when the job does not get done. I think that both labor and management have taken upon their shoulders the responsibility, and I wonder if this is not being too lenient on the worker who really does not catch the burnt of the responsibility for what has or has not been done.

Some of the more difficult problems to deal with concern the younger generation. I wonder what extent of the problems have to do with a difficulty in accepting responsibility and a difficulty in dealing with authority figures, the parental figures, be they of industry, labor, or the military.

Mr. Costaldo:

I believe that excesses beget excesses. I think that my generation was too easy on its children because we wanted them to have everything. As a result, we find ourselves with tremendous problems.

Audience:

My experience has been with the Drug and Hospital Workers' Union. The health care field is now a part of industry. Our only end-product, however, is the patient, a sick human being. The responsibilities to the patient are something that the union members have yet to learn. They know every paragraph in the bargaining agreement; they know it to their advantage. Insofar as absenteeism goes, I am only concerned with the misuse of days off or sick leave.

When an employee is sick, he should not be in the hospital working. Nevertheless, a hospital operates 365 days per year, seven days a week, twenty-four hours a day, and when an individual takes a hospital job, he should bear this in mind.

As management, we have always bargained in good faith. Nevertheless, every time we run across a labor problem, we are threatened by walk-outs. Walk-outs in hospitals are more serious than in any other work situation. I think that it is time that we start to teach individuals what their obligations are when they come to work in a hospital.

Mr. Lang:

When discussing problems concerning employees, I think it is important to remember that statistics implicate relatively few employees as irresponsible in this regard. Statistics show that only 10 percent of the work force constitutes 90 percent of the absences. The greater number of people are actually dedicated workers who feel just exactly as management would want them to feel.

Audience:

In addressing the problem of absenteeism, we are forgetting several things. What we should do is consider what kinds of programs we have to control absenteeism at our particular individual sites or locations. We should also look at these programs from the viewpoint of whether the absenteeism that occurs is excused or unexcused. The real problem rests with the irresponsible absentee, the individual who takes a day here and a day there. I think that the union can help in this regard by ignoring grievances from these individuals.

Audience:

I would like to make the point that motivation is directly related to absenteeism. There are job enrichment programs already in existence which large corporations are looking at and attempting to use, limited only by the regimentation due to union contracts. If the people at the top of unions and management were to get together to discuss absenteeism and jointly implement one of these programs, we would be much better off.

General Foods recently used a department of one of their plants to demonstrate that they could improve their attendance record. What they did was rotate the employees through the various jobs to see what kind of motivation would result. Their results were most encouraging.

Mr. Costaldo:

What they did was to involve the employees.

Dr. Gerstle:

Let us not lose sight of one fact. Why do people work? What motivation do they have? If someone has to work to eat he will probably think twice about being absent. (I speak here of the unexpected, unauthorized absence.) If an individual does not care, he will feel no compunction about staying away from work. The fact that people with so-called handicaps have less absenteeism and are on the whole above the average worker bears this out.

On the other hand, sometimes an employee has obligations at home which are not apparent to management or to the personnel director. A man may have a wife who is mentally ill, but not ill enough to be hospitalized. The man has to stay home, but he will not admit the true reason to his employer; as a result, this looks like unauthorized absenteeism.

Audience:

Most employers have realized by now that every case must be treated individually. All cases cannot be handled in the same way.

In addition, it has been found that if management wants the sick time record or accident rate to decrease, representatives must work toward that goal. It is necessary to work for it, to bring it to the forefront, and to make everyone aware of what the goal is.

Mr. Diamond:

The program I am involved with is an industrial alcoholism program. The Sanitation Department in New York City allows unlimited sick leave to its uniformed force. The fifty-two men in the Department's Alcoholism Program were absent a total of 2353 fewer days during the year after they entered the program, as compared to the prior year.

The program began as a strictly alcoholism-oriented program. It has now developed into the Employee's Assistance Program. Any individual not performing up to expectations at work can come to us and we will find the resources to help him with any family or personal problem. We have seen a decrease in absenteeism for alcoholics, and we hope to show a similar decrease for employees with other problems.

Audience:

I am unclear as to the respective roles of management and unions in dealing with problems such as alcoholism which cause absenteeism.

Mr. Costaldo:

An employee who abuses drugs or alcohol will often find it necessary to stay away from his job because of this overuse. It is quite possible, however, for an employee to hide such a problem for several years. Eventually the absenteeism may become chronic.

Management must take the first step in dealing with the individual. He has been hired by management to produce, and he is not producing. In addition, his work load is added to that of his fellow employees. When other workers complain, the union becomes involved and tries to handle the problem.

If the union has a progressive program, the individual is referred to some kind of treatment facility. Management is alerted and made aware of the problem and of what is being done. It is the joint concern of management and organized labor to help the individual and his family. If we do not help him, he will eventually become unemployed and therefore an additional tax load.

Question:

Is alcoholism the main cause of absenteeism?

Mr. Costaldo:

No, but it is a serious cause in my estimation. Drug abuse is another. In addition, the attitude toward work today has changed for the worse. We have to work at reversing this trend. Next, any employee needs a certain amount of dignity. That means education.

Question:

Does the union come to grips with the problem of absenteeism when it results from something other than alcoholism? Or do you feel that this is management's prerogative?

Mr. Costaldo:

Management must pinpoint the absenteeism if it gets to the point at which it is interfering with production. The only time the union can take action is when the members of the union complain to the union representative that they are doing the work of an absent individual. Then the union calls a meeting, talks to the absentee employee, and tries to get him some help.

Mr. Lang:

In other words, when an individual reaches the point of excessive absenteeism, the union enters the picture.

Mr. Costaldo:

Yes, but management usually pinpoints the problem for us. Management notifies the union before they feel it necessary to fire the employee. They try to find out why he is chronically absent; then, they talk to us. It is the union's job to deal effectively with the employee and see that he is helped.

In summary, unions and management must work together in dealing with the chronically absent employee and in dealing with absenteeism in general.

Chapter 5

THE ABSENTEE'S INITIAL CONTACT: THE FAMILY PHYSICIAN

CLEMENT J. BOCCALINI*

THE OPPORTUNITY to reflect on the extent and depth of involvement of the family physician in industry, and particularly in absenteeism, is a rare one for the family doctor. He is involved to a greater extent than just that of the physician of initial contact. His input varies greatly and depends upon his wish to participate, along with several factors beyond his control.

The use of a family physician as the initial contact and entry into the health system can usually limit or lessen delay or anxiety to the patient and check the mounting cost of medical services. A family physician is more inclined to cooperate on his patient's behalf if he knows what is going on about him at all levels and at all times.

The environment that surrounds that family doctor's patient at work is sometimes a nebulous one. In his many areas of expertise, occupational medicine is the one most often misunderstood by him. Too often there is evidence of competition when cooperation would better serve the interests of the employee. When the employee is becoming an absentee problem, and when this problem could be nipped in the bud, we instead see a blossoming of discord. Distrust develops and nourishes itself with the ignorance of simple facts.

---

*Clement J. Boccalini, M.D., F.A.A.F.P., is a family physician in private practice, certified by the American Board of Family Practice. President of the New York State Academy of Family Physicians, Dr. Bocaalini has been involved in industrial medicine as plant physician for the Sperry Gyroscope Corporation and has been medical consultant to the Board of Cooperative Educational Services. He is an Associate Professor of Clinical Family Medicine, State University of New York at Stony Brook.

As an example, when an employer or his agents refer an employee to a doctor, clinic, or emergency room several mechanisms are set in motion. The employee-patient is concerned with the best care he can get for his money. Obviously, all should be concerned with the best interests of the employee. An absentee problem arises when a decision should be arrived at equitably but is not. When a patient is physically ill with the well-established periods of disability as have been determined by experience, the problem is administratively simple. However, when discord results from psychological or emotional overtones, the problem becomes complex, especially when it compounds a serious illness.

The attitude of the physician at first contact is colored by the circumstances which surround his initial medical intervention. The type of relationship which takes place in the brief, urgent encounter, without any intent upon the part of the patient and the doctor to continue that relationship, is a very shallow one. Unfortunately, absenteeism due to anxiety and delay is increased by this type of approach.

The patient's attitude toward his employer, his supervisor, or his fellow employees greatly affects his wishes to return to work as quickly as possible. Based upon his experiences in the past with any of the above, or based on the various rumors that flow from the corridors or from desk to desk, an absent employee either looks forward to his return or finds a valid reason for not returning so quickly. He compares notes with others, he seeks advisors, calendars are consulted, and seasons considered. Is it purely coincidental that some absentee records denote a seasonal preference for weekends or holiday seasons?

Even when it is obvious, the company is rendered almost powerless by the "M.D. note." I am ashamed for those physicians who permit their patients to choose the date to return to work, almost as much as for those who repeatedly oblige the absentee by lengthening the periods of disability without offering reasonable explanations. To me it is unconscionable for an employee, particularly one in a municipal post, to be permitted medical leaves of long duration on the barest pretext. Notes without diagnosis or explanation of a request for medical leave are honored to reward people for "sick time accumulated." This type of subterfuge should not be tolerated. Fortunately, the insurance carriers who deal with industrial corporations have better fiscal approaches, and the medical departments do try to control indiscretions. What they cannot control, however, are orders from higher authorities in the organization, who arbitrarily make judgments.

An absent employee who does not have a favorable attitude at home with his family and friends or towards improving his health may become worse at home. He may not enjoy his home surroundings or the people in it, whether they be in-laws, dissident children, or a nagging spouse. He might do better away from home but not necessarily under the stresses of work. Frequently, however, physicians do recommend that their patients return to work during treatment and as a part of treatment. I feel that outside physicians should visit or make inquiries about the environment the patient works in, and I extend this especially to include psychiatrists and family physicians.

It is not easy to differentiate between the guilty appearance of some patients and the self-pity they manifest when they try to justify their requests for time off. Some have learned from past experiences that staying out a little longer is not too difficult. Some individuals with relatively minor illnesses can stretch the period of convalescence to a comfortable, brief vacation. It is not too difficult for malingerers to enjoy several brief vacations, and if the company medical department is not alert, no one becomes the wiser until the obvious pattern emerges. The slightest illness, a cold, acute gastritis, a headache is added to an uncomfortable working area or unwanted job and parleyed into a sick leave of respectable length. The true malingerer uses any available occasion for his won purposes.

On the other hand, some people seek out their physician in hopes that he will find some minor illness that can be readily eradicated by magic medicine. They know that they are not well and if questioned thoroughly will admit that their complaints may be stemming from the uncertainty of their employment or the difficulty of their work. When they begin to see flaws in their own achievements, they lose assurance in their own abilities. Belief in oneself is necessary for well-being. When fellow workers and supervisors confirm this feeling of lack of skill, surroundings become unbearable. A negative mental attitude follows. If the ability to adapt lessens, stress and its many consequences occur, and this pressure takes its toll in chronic illnesses. Those unable to cope further with an illness add to this absentee fold. Many defer seeking the advice of a doctor. But avoiding medical attention aggravates the illness far beyond its usual progress. In the course of periodic examinations, one must almost become a preacher to convince some employees of their need for preventive or early treatment.

In all of the above circumstances the family physician should be included, step-by-step, and from the very beginning. He should be involved in any medical evaluation or recommendation of treatment, no matter how small or how large. The family doctor should not be left out on the perimeter. He should be in the hub of any circle of such activity. If he is dedicated to the total welfare of his patient, he must be involved. Employees should not be permitted to evaluate their own illnesses nor set the standards of care. They should be participants. They should not dictate medical policy, nor should management seek ways to circumvent the decisions of a medical opinion.

Plant medical departments should be autonomous. They should set the rules and exceptions. Any peer structure which permits management or labor in any of its diverse forms to pressure, threaten, or cajole the medical department causes more problems than the solutions it seeks. From a practical viewpoint, it knowingly permits disrespect, lowers professional morale, and eventually raises the premiums. If this type of problem exists, consider it a cause for much more concern as time goes on.

One source of dicomfort is the employee who can manage to manipulate his friends and sometimes his family into accepting his sickness in a major light. Soon he becomes able to convince those in authority to listen to his sad plea. When the employer or management or the company doctor can be presented as villains, sympathy and eventually the support of the personal physician is gained.

Give time and the probing of the wife or husband and children, an employee will seek the services of his family physician; though this might not be the initial contact, it might very well be the point of initiation into a detailed health care pattern. Most family doctors comply and cooperate with requests for information. Most are desirous of helping their patients return to gainful employment.

However, there are those doctors who consider any employer as a monster corporation that treats their patients poorly. The list of physicians who feel this way, fortunately, is diminishing rapidly. More and more physicians, whether they are aware of it or not, are joining the ranks of the employed themselves as school physicians, insurance examiners, and consultants for agencies and corporations. Yet the specter of St. George fighting the dragon seems to appear whenever the physician is convinced that an employer is taking advantage of his patient. Defending the underdog is the sporting thing to do.

I stated before that the patient sometimes decides the date of his return to work. This is a conclusion I have come to from the discussions and admissions of many employees returning with notes signed many weeks since their last visit to any doctor. It is less liable to be the case if the family doctor sees them more frequently. However, doctors working in hospitals where less time can be devoted to the many aspects of personalized medicine are more apt to succumb to this approach, especially if they delegate these duties to their aides. Let us remember that many older family physicians are individualists who object to writing forms and answering requests because it interferes with their set ways. But those who have kept up with the active practice of medicine cannot in good conscience serve their patients well unless they are willing to take the few moments needed to fill out medical forms.

School physicians are well aware of the type of unfounded requests received for special services. I have asked some colleagues to explain their approaches to these requests. In almost every instance the doctor admitted his reluctance to make such requests in writing and also admitted that he had to appease the patient or parent. At first it is done hesitantly, then automatically and without knowledge of what is implied in the request. Medical excuses for time lost are one step removed from this approach. The line between cooperation and convenient expediency is a thin one, especially since we are in most cases dealing with the breadwinner.

In most cases I believe that this contribution to prolonged absenteeism could be reduced dramatically in many instances. It requires a coordinated bipartisan type approach with mutually understood confidence shared. To put this into effect one must first admit that there is a gap in communication and then come to an understanding of why this gap is so wide. We should recognize readily the need to submit to discussion to differences or, better still, sharing confidences. The family physician should not be in awe of the corporate structure, nor should the medical department be made to become a rubber stamp. The family physician's cooperation should be sought and welcomed by industry because with both working towards a common goal, absenteeism would be reduced. Though the family physician may be the one to initially or subsequently best treat the absentee, he is not necessarily capable of deciding the extent of employability his patient has attained at that particular point in time and in the specific area of his work.

The place of the family physician in industrial medicine is widely disagreed upon, as shown in the following example. Recently, an advisory committee of the New York State Workmen's Compensation Board stated that "the family doctor is not especially involved to any great degree with occupational injury and disease." Some officials are ostriches when it comes to accepting innovative ideas.

A newly published book on family practice came out recently. It is a comprehensive book which promises to become the basic text for determining a curriculum in family medicine and in preparation for the Specialty Board Examinations. Though man subspecialties were not included, an entire chapter was devoted to occupational medicine.

The editor of the Official Journal of Air Traffic Control Medicine is airing a similar battle in which he notes that, "To deny the central problem of occupational stress when this aspect is so obviously, volubly, persistently, explicitly, intrinsically, and explosively perceived by employees, supervisors, writers, legislators, and physicians is to refuse to take notice. Those who suffer the real pains of an ulcer become even more tense when management denies the common sense observations of the rest of humanity."

Most of the illnesses treated in industry are those of upright patients receiving ambulatory care. Dr. Charles Houston of the University of Vermont, College of Medicine, recently claimed that the walking sick and the worried well constitute 90 percent of all office patients. He points out that the worried well are a reflection of our times. Whereas four years ago the National Health Bill was three billion dollars, it is now increased by an added one hundred thirty million dollars. Yet this area of care has received the least attention from medical planners despite the fact that these are the greatest contributors to absenteeism and loss of income. Family practice is focusing on ambulatory care where the needs are; it always has. What happens to his patient at work should be as important to the family physician as industry's interest in the other two thirds of a man's lifetime.

When one peruses the medical reports and excuses for absence, one has to wonder whether the notes were intended to be accepted without being read. Rarely does the private physician take the brief time required to write a note in depth describing his findings or the diagnosis in full. The most common offenses appear on the DS 450 form, which should be completed before the date of return. Symptoms and other subjective complaints are inserted after the word "diagnosis" while "dates" are answered by the overworked term undetermined." Most often, when the date of return to work is completed, an accompanying note requests part time light duty. When questioned, the doctor will often admit that he does not know the extent of strain or fatigue encountered during the working day.

These are minor hurdles. They become major obstacles when it becomes evident that we are dealing with psychiatric disorders or problems of abuse. Barriers still exists in medicine when dealing with alcoholism in industry. Though it may be the largest single behavioral problem that faces industry today, only a small fraction of the thousands of corporations are seriously involved with alcoholism programs.

There are millions of job holders abusing this drug, knowingly becoming antisocial and diseased. Such a man threatens his life and his health. The safety of all whom he encounters, even by chance is endangered. Though it is the most treatable chronic disease, it remains untreated, discreetly hidden under other diagnoses, and permitted to flourish. When doctors bravely write "alcoholism" as clearly as they now write "Abortion" on a patient's records, the first forward step will be taken.

If we are talking about absenteeism with an intent to reduce it, let us start the job with alcoholism. This is an area in which the family physician can make a reasonable contribution. It starts with calling a spade a spade and not a virus. The employer's wishes must be respected, but only to a limited point. The company medical department may not be the treatment place of his choice since what is being sought is for the mutual good of the many involved; all should have some knowledge of what is being accomplished. The employer has the most persuasive argument to bind the pact—job security. This cannot continue to be an empty threat if it is to be of any major consequence in the long run.

There are other major areas in which absenteeism can be reduced. Long absences for chronic or malignant diseases are most times not only justified but necessary, but blanket disability for a chronic condition with renewed absences interspersed between short unproductive periods of work should not be encouraged. When such an employee is burdened beyond his capacities, his usefulness quickly diminishes. To have him return to a job at which his fellow employees may deride him adds insult to injury. And magnanimous gestures on the part of management or labor merely prolong the downhill course.

The need for improved communications between the family physician and the employee's personnel or medical department has been mentioned. Getting the forms filled out and returned is becoming more difficult as more and more paperwork is being added to the practice of medicine. Busy men refer this chore to lesser knowledgeable aides or delay it. For many it is not fiscally feasible to hire help for the express purpose of handling third party forms.

We have discussed here the difficulties brought about in our relationships by first, the attitudes of the employee-patient-absentee and second, his relationships to his job, community, home, family, and his own positive or negative contributions. The relationship he has with his doctor and the role his family physician wishes to assume is the third leg of this tripod. If it is not a supporting one, he will be missing the encouragement he needs to endure illnesses.

The attitude of the doctor at the point of initial contact is determined either by intent or chance. When the physician has declared his intent and has taken the time and means to develop this ability, we realize that we are witnessing a new approach. Many patients consider any physician they see on a personal basis along with another member of their family as the family doctor. Many physicians render good primary care in general areas regardless of their specialty. However, if they are trained in a specialty by intent and education, then they become family physicians either by chance or by default of their specialty.

For generations, each member of a family traditionally sought out the family doctor as soon as any need for medical attention arose. Though the patterns of living have changed, including the behavior of members in or outside of a family unit, the seeking of a personal physician is an attempt to return to earlier times. At the moment of his greatest need for help, this benevolent time machine, as he sees it, returns him to the security of earlier experiences.

The emphasis in family practice today is to regain that confidence by assuring medical security at all times, to all members, and for all reasons. It does not imply that the family physician becomes an expert in all fields of specialty training, but he must be able to recognize the need for and judge the proficiency of each treatment his patient receives. This approach offers a comprehensive, continuing, coordinated community care without regard to sex, age, disease, or organ. The family physician oversees the care of the patient throughout his total needs. He does not replace or eliminate any other specialty but is judiciously involved in all medical needs of his patients. There are those who forsee him as the keystone in future medical service groups. Not to involve the family doctor in occupational or industrial health planning is to exclude the professional who statistically has been taking care of the majority of ills directly and at other times has been showing expert attention to those not within his own area. Thus, the family physician directs the employee into a medical system from the moment of initial contact, and he becomes the employee's medical counsel by remaining involved.

If an employee is fortunate enough to have such medical care he will want his doctor contacted for all his ills, and it is the obligation of anyone acting as the employee's agent to do so. Any temporary difficulty in communication does not alter the propriety and advisability that the physician be notified. In emergencies, the immediate best care for the employee is paramount in importance. The family physician must in turn offer pertinent information about his patient so that the medical personnel can act on the patient's behalf or in cooperation with the physician's request. This is especially important when employees are unwilling to communicate or are unaware of their own disabilities.

Means of better informing physicians about the most common problems handled by a company's medical department would go far in showing cooperation. This could be done on a formal scale by scheduling workshops or by releasing bulletins in the myriad journals that reach us. I receive journals every day of the week in large bulk, and I try to read as many of them as I can. I rarely see anything, however, which tells the family doctor much about industrial medicine. There are books and magazines concerned with industrial medicine, but none of these are directed towards the family physician. Workshops, journal articles, or interspecialty meetings would be a partial solution to this problem.

In conclusion, it is noted that industry is vitally concerned with its ability to meet planned productivity goals. When any element within the corporate structure threatens the delay of this schedule, the causes must be found and corrections instituted promptly.

Absenteeism is such a threat of major magnitude about which more has been said than accomplished. Questionable medical reports should be thoroughly investigated and valuable working time thus gained. A medical judgment should not be disregarded, or worse, countermanded by any indelicate show of favoritism. Similarly, the lack of an adhered to policy leaves much to be desired. Problems should be met head-on beyond the suspicion of favoritism. The family physician is in a unique position to establish a smooth liaison medically and emotionally between an absentee employee and a corporation's personnel and medical departments. His involvement should be continuous and cooperative in the sharing of responsibility.

DISCUSSION

Panelists in this discussion were experts in family and industrial medicine and included George J. Adler, M.D., Vice Chairman, Education Commission, New York State Academy of Family Physicians; Clement J. Boccalini, M.D., President-Elect, New York State Academy of Family Physicians; and J. C. Duffy, M.D., Medical Director of International Business Machines Corporation. Robert P. Jessup, M.D., is Medical Director of Grumman Aerospace Corporation; Louis A. Lanzetta, M.D., is Medical Director of the New York City Transit Authority; Morton G. Miller, M.D., is Associate Professor, Department of Psychiatry, Health Sciences Center of the State University of New York at Stony Brook. Other panelists were Melville G. Rosen, M.D., Professor, Department of Family Medicine at Stony Brook; Daniel J. Sullivan, M.D., Associate Medical Director, Metropolitan Life Insurance Company; and Eileen Waters, R.N., Medical Department, National Bank of North America.

Question:

Is it a family, home, or personal adjustment problem that leads to a job adjustment problem, or is it the job adjustment problem that aggravates personal and family relationships?

Dr. Miller:

I do not believe that there is any good data in the psychiatric literature which would answer this question. As I see such problems in a clinical setting, I am led to the conclusion that such situations interact, and it is very difficult to pinpoint definite causation. In good clinical practice, one has to examine cases on an individual basis. I have found, however, that most physicians and psychiatrists tend to underestimate the significance of job problems in assessing individual pathology.

Question:

The family physician, to be effective, should be interested in the environment in which his patients work. What kind of contact should the family doctor have with management, and what are the ways and means used to obtain this sort of information?

Dr. Boccalini:

I feel that the company medical director is in the position to offer such an interchange of information. He should invite the family doctor to come in or call in and discuss his patient when there is any uncertainty as to how long an employee should stay out of work. Discussions should focus specifically on the requirements and environment of the job in question; in addition, this discussion should offer mutual enlightenment.

Dr. Jessup:

In my own experience, I have had a great deal of difficulty in convincing family physicians to come into the plant to view the work environment. I often call an employee's family doctor to give him my viewpoint of his patient's problems.

Dr. Duffy:

I think that the occupational physician has an additional responsibility. If there is a potential environmental exposure, the company physician should advise the family doctor of his suspicions and recommendations for possible method of treatment.

Also, the occupational physician has the responsibility of being active in medical societies and of maintaining hospital staff affiliations. This will give him the opportunity to prevent his viewpoint and further the education of physicians in the community.

Dr. Lanzetta:

As Medical Director for the New York City Transit Authority, I am responsible for 38,000 employees. I have found that the family physician treats an individual as a patient and not as an employee. There seems to be a tendency for the family doctor to increase the convalescence period beyond that thought advisable by our own medical department without even inquiring into the type of work the individual does. We in the medical department are in the position to change a man's job from a strenuous activity to a desk job when he is recovering from a serious illness or accident. However, because the personal physician has already decided that the employee should stay out of work, we do not often have the opportunity.

Audience:

It has occurred to me that when an employee goes to his doctor's office with the disability form, he could very easily bring a job description statement from the personnel office as well. This would give the family physician an idea of what the individual actually does and would help in determining convalescence periods.

Dr. Boccalini:

This is an excellent suggestion. At present, there is a tremendous lack of communication between company and family physcians. This has become a barrier to solving many problems and should not be allowed to continue.

Dr. Jessup:

It is not only the family physician who is to be criticized for his lack of interest in his patients' occupations, but also first line supervisors for their ignorance of employees' lives away from the job. Just as, perhaps, the family physician does not inquire to any depth into the patient's job, the first line supervisor in too many cases has no idea of what the employee's home life is like or what his problems are. It is the unusual supervisor who takes the time to know his people and their problems. This would go a long way towards opening up communication and towards solving a great deal of absenteeism problems.

We are not discussing only pure health absenteeism. We are thinking of the selected, the unannounced and the alcoholic days off as well. Too many times I have consulted a first line supervisor who knows nothing about a given employee's background, claiming that he is too busy. Supervisors must get to know their subordinates if we are to come any closer to solving their problems.

Dr. Adler:

I would like to discuss the family physician's point of view. I think that almost every conscientious family physician is well aware of the effects of job pressures on his patients' health. Most family physicians are attuned to psychological factors and do make an inquiry of sorts as to sources of tension and conflict both in the home and at work. When there is a persistent problem, the personal physician is usually able to isolate major areas of tension. As a family physician, I would initiate a discussion of job problems if this seems to me to be the main area of tension production.

In fact, this is not so much a discussion of the patient's problems as it is a ventilation of his complaints. Family physicians serve a very unique role in the psychiatric care of their patients by being interested listeners. Many such doctors actually set time aside for "talking appointments" after ruling out organic pathology. Such time is used so that the patient can complain and discuss job pressures. Sometimes just talking about it can ease the problem. Occasionally, the interested family physician will go to the employer or the personnel director to seek more information and to try to work with them. This is rare, however, mainly because of the pressures of the physician's own patient load.

One of the major differences in emphasis between the industrial physician and the family physician is evident in decisions about return to work dates and filling out of forms. First of all, there are certain factors present in the home situation of which the industrial physician is not aware, but which do complicate the patient's return to normal functioning. There are definite secondary gain factors operating in favor of the patient. A very important consideration is medical-legal responsibility. For instance, a doctor would certainly rather make an error on the side of conservatism when deciding when a coronary patient can return to work. Because of the different requirements of the jobs of industrial and family physician, there is a different emphasis on psychological and return-to-work factors.

Dr. Sullivan:

Many times artificial situations are created because of the involvement of a third party such as management or union. Contracts often include clauses which are very difficult to apply to reality; absenteeism with full disability payments is one such example. The company tries to enforce this clause by asking the family physician whether the employee is fully disabled and unable to work. The individual may not be totally disabled and therefore not entitled to disability payments. However, the family physician may feel that the individual is nevertheless unable to return to work. There are so many vague situations which require precise decisions. Perhaps an individual is not entitled to full disability payments but should be given a leave of absence. Too often such situations are not covered in contracts.

On the other hand, the contract may be so binding and the mechanisms so involved that the layman who administers the plan in a particular factory or plant may be unable or unwilling to administer the plan correctly. A person who needs a leave of absence to straighten out some problems may never receive the opportunity because of a complex contract.

Dr. Rosen:

As we progress technologically, industry is very interested in its own gain but is also trying to maintain some interest in the behavior of employees. In the final analysis, however, there are certain rigid guidelines set legally by unions, government, and third party carriers that even the most sensitive physician finds himself in the middle of and in which he must try to find loopholes if he is to work in the best interest of his patients. On top of all this is the basic human chemistry of the individual who is not completely honest because he sees other people getting away with things.

The family physician necessarily becomes involved in all this as soon as he must fill out a company disability form. If he writes that a woman must be out of work because of unbearable pressures in the home, the diagnosis will not be accepted by industry as allowable. When I personally make a diagnosis, I like to diagnose the behavioral aspect of an illness. However, the psychiatric or psychosomatic aspect of disease is not as well accepted by industry as is the precise physical problem, and many doctors are therefore forced to lie in order to do what is best for their patients.

By the same token, the honest family physician will discourage his patients from using sick days that they really do not need.

Audience:

As a superintendent of schools, I am not quite in industry and do not have the profit motives that might be evident in a corporation. I have had problems with the opposite of absenteeism. Occasionally, we have to relieve a teacher of classroom duties because he or she can no longer control the class. We refer this teacher to his family physician, and in a relatively short time we are told that the teacher is ready to return to work, that it will be therapeutic for him. My own feeling is that it may be good for the teacher to get back to work, but it will not be good for the students in his classroom, and that is where my responsibility lies. I find myself in the position, then, of encouraging absenteeism.

Dr. Duffy:

I am convinced that the vast majority of people are motivated to come to work. It is the obligation of personnel departments, occupational health programs, and family physicians to try and identify early in their employment the chronic problem individuals with attitudinal disturbances. I am sure that these individuals with their repeated minor complaints are as exasperating to personal physicians as they are to the industrial organization.

It is only through a cooperative effort to identify the problem type early in employment that one can try to get these individuals straightened out and ready to be good employees.

Dr. Rosen:

Such a cooperative effort would lead to less absenteeism and fewer problems in the home. Individuals, such as Civil Service employees and teachers with tenure cannot be fired. Without a doubt, these individuals eventually become unhappy in their jobs and at home, affecting family life. I believe that if industry paid more attention to this type of situation, we would have a better distribution of the work force in positions where they are motivated and excited about the present and future.

Ms. Waters:

I feel that too many of our employees return to work too early because they cannot stand being at home for an extended period of time. They convince their personal physicians that they are ready to come back to work; as a result, most of these employees go back on disability shortly thereafter. When I feel that an employee has returned to work too quickly, I generally keep in contact with him and his progress.

Dr. Lanzetta:

I have found that when an employee has no sick days left, he is extremely anxious to get back to work, even if he is not yet ready.

Question:

Occasionally, a patient asks me to sign a disability form stating that he must be out for six months when there is really nothing wrong with him. Aside from the fact that I am morally opposed to such a practice, I have declined on the basis that a false diagnosis would never get through the medical department of the organization. Is it possible that a disability form falsified in such a way could get through the medical department of the organization and be processed for disability payments?

Dr. Lanzetta:

At the Transit Authority we have medical consultants who check every diagnosis so that falsified forms will not be processed. However, it is conceivable that an individual could receive six months of disability payments when nothing is wrong with him if his company did not check up on him.

Dr. Sullivan:

I have found that by simply going back to the personal physician who signed the form and asking specific questions about the diagnosis I have been able to eliminate many false disability forms. The family physician frequently lets me know that he signed the form under duress.

Question:

Occasionally, a family physician tells me that the reason an employee has been absent so much is that he is an alcoholic. However, the physician will not sign any forms or statements claiming that the employee is an alcoholic. How can this situation be dealt with?

Dr. Boccalini:

I would immediately send the employee to our counselling service, just on the suspicion of alcoholism. He would not be fired.

Dr. Lanzetta:

As soon as the alcoholic employee goes to the counselling service we remove him from his job if he is a busman or motorman. He is placed in a desk job. We do not fire alcoholics. As long as the alcoholic employee attends counselling sessions, he is kept on the job.

Question:

What if the individual were on methadone?

Dr. Lanzetta:

Unfortunately, we could not accept for employment an individual on methadone. This is partly because of the negative feelings of the public and partly because I do not feel that the methadone patient's reflexes are all intact.

Dr. Sullivan:

One reason for the difference in policy for the alcoholic and the methadone maintained individual is that the alcoholic is an old, trusted employee while the methadone patient is generally a new employee.

Dr. Lanzetta:

The most compelling reason that I know of for not employing individuals who are on methadone is that these individuals do not always stick to methadone and occasionally abuse other drugs.

Dr. Adler:

I would like to discuss the question of doctors "covering up" for patients, particularly alcoholic patients. In general, doctors are an honest and responsible group of people. We have an allegiance to our patients, and occasionally this allegiance leads us to "cover up" for patients without actually being dishonest.

For instance, I would be happy to write that Mr. X has been sick with gastritis without adding that it was an alcoholic gastritis. If the medical department wishes to discuss this with me in more detail and my patient has signed a release so that I can discuss his physical condition, I will explain Mr. X's problem completely. However, I am in no way obligated to be an informant on my patient to government or industry.

Dr. Boccalini:

When a patient signs a release of information form, I would make it clear to him that the information is being passed on so that he can be helped by the company counselling service, for instance. If the patient does not sign the release form, his doctor must make a decision. He must decide when to keep a patient's condition hidden and when to be as honest as he can with the company medical department in order to keep his patient's problem from becoming more serious.

Dr. Lanzetta:

If I thought that my patient were going to lose his job because of something I could tell the company medical department, I would keep his condition to myself, with one exception. If the combination of the illness and his remaining on the job were detrimental to his life, I would certainly inform the company.

Audience:

I would submit that in any case where you have an alcoholism program in industry, it is necessary to threaten job loss to motivate an employee into treatment. Keeping his condition secret would seem to defeat the purpose.

Dr. Sullivan:

A company with an alcoholism program should certainly be kept informed of all alcoholic employees. It is the small organization which would immediately fire the alcoholic that we are concerned about.

Dr. Duffy:

Management has employed the individual to do a productive job and has a sincere interest in his continuing health. When the family physician is aware that a patient is drinking himself to death and does not initiate a contact with an employer to establish some sort of program for the benefit of the employee, this doctor is not doing the patient a service. He is only assisting in the concealment of the problem and the further damage to the patient's health.

Audience:

I would not expect an employee's personal physician to go out of his way to inform me that one of my employees is an alcohlic. I think that if our supervision is so poor that we have not picked this up or if the employee is still performing well, there is no sense in our being informed of the problem. In other words, I believe that it is industry's responsibility to discover such problems through observation of job performance and absenteeism patterns.

Dr. Rosen:

Again, this all comes down to individualization. My responsibility is to my patient. Alcoholism is a condition which requires treatment. I often find that if a patient does not accept treatment programs, I can motivate him or force him into a treatment program by threatening to tell his employer that he is an alcoholic.

Some industries would actually be disturbed if an employee did not have a few drinks at lunch when closing a business deal. For instance, in the banking business, many big deals are made over a drink. Some district managers approve of this, and others do not. Recently, I examined an individual whose supervisor does not approve of drinking. Consequently, I will not tell the supervisor to what extent this employee drinks. However, if this employee resists treatment I will tell his supervisor that the man is an alcoholic. The supervisor will threaten the individual with job loss, and he will probably be convinced to enter a treatment program.

Question:

How does the family physician handle absenteeism which is not related to alcoholism or drug abuse, but which is indicated by many different kinds of complaints?

Dr. Boccalini:

The family doctor does not see this as absenteeism. Absenteeism is a term used by those who see a problem. The family physician is looking only at the care of his patient during a sick period of time.

Dr. Adler:

The family physician does not see an absenteeism problem, but sees a patient constantly coming to the office for a multitude of ailments, very few of which seem significant enough to warrant this much medical attention. Sometimes the physician will give a name to these little problems on the company medical form. Occasionally, however, we delve a little deeper and realize that there are psychological factors operating.

Dr. Boccalini:

In many cases, the family physician is not aware of the absenteeism pattern of his patient. For instance, some individuals take off the two days before or after a weekend and have someone else sign them in. When this is discovered, it is most profitable for the plant physician and family physician to work together.

Dr. Rosen:

Absenteeism in that case is a symptom of another condition, not always illness. Absenteeism can be due to other problems such as unhappiness with a job. The family physician should address himself to this situation.

Question:

What does the family physician do about signing a request for time off with company medical coverage when the patient's complaints are largely psychosomatic?

Dr. Boccalini:

Such requests are quite frequent. I feel that if a patient has an illness, the direction should be toward treating that illness. If the illness is psychosomatic, I will refer the patient to a specialist or bring in a consultant. If the patient refuses to go along with this, I will not sign the company form.

Dr. Adler:

I have had this sort of problem come up quite often. If I feel that a patient's disease is not organic but is psychogenic, I will handle the problem as a psychiatric one. In many ways, I feel that I am better equipped to deal with my patient than a psychiatrist would be since I have the benefit of previous experience with the patient.

I sometimes feel that, as part of the treatment, the individual should be removed from a tension producing setting. If I feel that his job is contributing to his condition, I will write a note to the personnel director stating that the patient is in a chronic tension state and that I have advised him to remain away from work for an unspecified time while I am treating him with supportive and medical therapy.

Question:

Suppose to your satisfaction, the work environment is not a factor in the patient's state. Do you feel justified in asking an insurance carrier and a corporation to cover this patient insurance-wise and absence-wise for a non-work connected problem?

Dr. Adler:

I will not put down a false diagnosis. I generally advise such an individual to stay away from the work environment so that I can evaluate him. If his job has nothing to do with his condition, I will not keep him out of work any longer. However, if I feel that the individual's psychological condition might hamper him in his work duties or might result in some sort of dangerous situation coming up, I will request that he be given a leave of absence.

Dr. Rosen:

I believe that industry is moving in the right direction as they are beginning to choose personnel to fit any particular job. As a result, people will be happier at work.

Physicians are also moving in the right direction in considering the behavioral aspects of disease. We are now developing educational programs for the sophisticated family physician. The new image of general practitioner is the well trained, competent individual who is sensitive to non-organic problems as well as to organic ones.

If industry continues to choose personnel who will be happy at their jobs and family physicians continue to be sensitive to the many needs of their patients, we will shortly find solutions to the problem of absenteeism.

Dr. Duffy:

In the final analysis, what is right for the individual is right for the corporation. Company medical departments are finding that working very closely with family physicians is in the best interests of everyone concerned.

Chapter 6

PSYCHIATRIC ASPECTS
OF ABSENTEEISM

JOHN MACIVER*

To ADEQUATELY DEAL WITH the problem of industrial absenteeism it is necessary to change attitudes, beliefs, and values of
both employers and employees in order that individuals may feel
better about themselves and their work. To be sure, this is no
small order.

Freud was once asked to state the chief ends of human existence. His answer covered a vast territory in five words: to love and
to work. This oft-quoted phrase forcefully indicates the central
position which work has in human life. Work should have a
spiritual dimension; that is, it should have meaning beyond the
economic.

Obviously all work is not the same. Any discussion of work
absence is not complete without a full account of the nature of the
work from which the employee is absent. In this country many
men and women find gratifying jobs; others do not. Our basic
task is to delineate the failures and deficiencies in the organization
of our work system which will throw light on its shortcomings for

---

*John MacIver, M.D., M.P.H., has enjoyed a distinguished career in psychiatry,
industrial medicine, and public health. He attended Harvard College and was
graduated from the College of Physicians and Surgeons of Columbia University. Dr.
MacIver took his residency in psychiatry at Yale University, where he also received
a Master's Degree in Public Health. For many years he has been actively involved
in industrial psychiatry. From 1960-1966 he was Assistant Medical Director of the
United States Steel Corporation and from 1966-1971 was Director of Psychiatric
Services. Dr. MacIver has also been on the Staff of Mt. Sinai Hospital in New York
and has sat on the faculties of the Department of Psychiatry and the Graduate
School of Public Health of the University of Pittsburgh. He is now in the private
practice of psychiatry in Hyannis, Massachusetts.

a significant percentage of our work force.

The commonly used term *absenteeism* has a pejorative ring. A large segment of unscheduled work absence is actually illness absence and is perfectly legitimate. With this redefinition the dimensions of the problem shrink. I prefer to use the term *absenteeism* to refer only to deviant problem absence.

This is not to say that this redefinition is universally accepted or inclusively accurate. What is needed are clear-cut, operational definitions to cover the various types of absence from work. In my definition, the Monday absence of the alcoholic is not included as absenteeism because it does not represent deviant absence, but rather a type of illness absence. Drug related absence is a similar case. Even those situations in which workers might have been able to work but did not, do not necessarily represent willful absence. This appears to be true especially among minority groups and the young.

Clinical examination of undependable workers will reveal much in the way of characterological disorder. Much depressive symptomatology and pervasive fearfulness result from exposure to new or novel situations, including work situations—much more so than is commonly realized. The plant or factory, or even office, may be a threatening place indeed. Accounts of the early family life of absence-prone minority group workers can make for grim listening. Ego and superego functions are often deficient in this population and commonly accepted work habits stressing industriousness, punctuality, and individual responsibility have never been well-developed.

The psychology of absence among the young is more subtle. Among this group ego functions may well appear normal, but there is a profound sense of alienation from establishment values and those values commonly accepted by the work force. These have individuals who are questioning themselves, their values and ours, their futures and ours. They are often not particularly happy or comfortable individuals (nor do they make us more traditional types particularly comfortable in their questioning of the status quo) .

The large more or less conventional group that remains is im-

portant and significant in any discussion of work absence, if only
in terms of numbers and potential productive capacity. They are
those tens of millions in the work force who are neither distinctly
psychiatrically ill nor impaired, and who also, by and large, cleave
to the major values held in our society (even if they hold them
uncomfortably to some extent). Our industrial system should be
organized to make work life more emotionally rewarding to this
mainstream or our work force, as well as to the supervisors and
managers who bear the great responsibility of directing the work
activity of others. Only if we better organize this great middle
American group will work absence *in toto* become more rational
and less deviant. This is not to say that work absence will necessarily be reduced in frequency or amount. Absence will not in the
long run be reduced by analytical studies which have as their goal
simply controlling absence "across the board." Sometimes absence
should in fact be encouraged. "Presentism" results when on-the-
job pressures prevent the taking of entitled vacation or when
supervisors and managers work when they should be at home in
bed.

Only when we carefully rethink the values and beliefs that
underlie work and its motivations do we move forward. In psychiatry symptoms are important and deserve attention. But discern-
ing and interpreting what lies behind symptoms is what really
leads to significant insights. So too with absenteeism. Absence is a
symptom. Underlying implications and significances must be investigated continuously as conditions change.

There are two types of industrial organization: adversary and
paternalistic (and inevitably, mixtures of these purer forms).
Both have advantages and drawbacks as vehicles for the channel-
ing of human effort. Both are to an unacceptable extent crippling
to the human spirit as we view human possibilities in a democratic society. Furthermore both modes of organization are based
on out-dated belief systems.

One knows where one stands in the adversary organization,
and there is no illusion that one need not protect himself at all
times. This mode may also accurately reflect the realities of a
hostile environment; as a result working in an adversary environ-

ment may be advantageously toughening. Among the disadvantages of the adversary mode, none is more vivid than the management-union split with the tremendous amount of energy expended in fighting behavior, with consequently diminished energy available for the commonwealth. Equally damaging are the effects on the individual. Managers learn to give employees only what is specified in the contract. Employees are commonly resentful, bitter, or apathetic.

The quality of mercy is indeed constrained in the adversary mode of organization. It is then not surprising to discern a general tendency to "beat the system" whenever possible. There is little feeling of shared needs and consequent working toward common goals. Dedication, teamwork, and the like are not greatly in evidence (although in the large organization there may be isolated pockets of high morale and efficiency). Deviant work behavior, including excessive absence, is controlled by external sanctions and punishments. The price paid in productive efficiency and human bitterness in the adversary organization is great.

The paternalistic mode of industrial organization offers numerous contrasts, and it has its own disadvantages. Paternalistic organizations wield their authority by over-emphasizing security needs and encouraging passive behavior. The typical employee psychological reaction is what is commonly known as hostile dependency. One is dependent but does not like the situation and therefore struggles against it. It is the proud boast of one paternalistically based giant industrial organization that not once in its one hundred year history has an employee been laid off. Employees in such a setting come to expect more and more as their due. The punch line of the familiar joke comes to mind: "But what have you done for me lately?"

Senator Charles Percy, former president of the Bell and Howell Company, recently stated that he believes we are on the brink of a "major breakthrough in an attempt to change ideas on work." While many breakthroughs actually turn out not to happen (such as the automation panic of the early 1960's) it is just possible that the millions of young people now entering the work force will bring about major changes in industrial organization and many of its implicit values. More young people were added to the work force in the 1960's than in any other decade in history. Going on the finding of several Gallup polls, it is safe to say that young people are particularly dissatisfied with their jobs. This poses a growing threat to United States industrial output. The now famous General Motors Lordstown strike was a reaction by predominantly young male adults to what they considered dehumanizing output demands. Whether this is a straw in the wind, a portent of the future, no one can say for sure.

Senator Percy places the blame for job dissatisfaction on "an entrenched authoritarian industrial system that has taken decades and decades to build." These are rather strong words in referring to an industrial system that has produced an unprecedented cornucopia of goods and services. Because of the system's very productivity we are left with some rather difficult choices.

Once again referring to the Senator's remarks, he said, "There is a strong feeling that managerial and labor institutions have sometimes grown too rigid. Too often they have become blind to the broader needs of our society." Senator Percy accurately perceives the two sides of the problem. Both labor and management would do well to change their outdated strategies and tactics. But can they? Can industrial systems change so that we can produce more with more gratification and a greater feeling of being on the same team, serving the same cause? There will certainly never be a better time than the present to make the attempt.

With the tremendous wealth of knowledge and understanding in the behavioral sciences which have accumulated in the twentieth century, this is an ideal time to reshape our ideas on industrial organization. There is a tremendous research investment in industry directed toward improved production methods, new products and services, and even a touch of basic research, but there is virtually nothing in the way of in-house research or investment in the behavioral-organizational area. An important reason for the dearth of research is that executives who can make policy decisions along these lines to implement such research are themselves psychologically threatened by this area. Too many of our nation's leaders have been too successful as achievers in the framework of existing values to see the need for or the potential for change. This is a most difficult problem. With their firmly held values and with the *status quo* reinforcement of their own achievements, it is next to impossible to convince industrial leaders that there are other legitimate sets of values held in many segments of American society.

A valuable concept formulated in the early 1960's, but perhaps never worked out in sufficient detail, may provide us with a positive course to follow. The concept is known as "reciprocation," and it was advanced by Dr. Harry Levinson of the Harvard Business School. Briefly, in a work situation a person is a member of an organization, which has certain minimal conditions which must be met if one is to remain a member. Similarly, that person requires of the organization minimal guarantees of a certain kind.

Work life also involves other people in the group. They demand of the individual that he contribute to the group purpose and that he respond via the ways of behaving that are traditionally acceptable in that group. At the same time, the person demands of the group that he be recognized as someone with an individual, unique identity. The company, therefore, consists of the reciprocal relationships between the company and the individual as well as between the work group and the individual.

A third area of reciprocation involves the work task. The task has its own formal requirements, and the individual brings to the task capacities, skills, and interests which permit him to fulfill these requirements. Thus, the reciprocation process involves all of the aspects of work life within an organization.

From these reciprocal relationships emerge the expectations which people hold about the company, their work group, and their tasks. The company also has expectations of its people, as expressed in policies and practices, and in varying degrees, the people are aware of these expectations. Out of this evolves the concept of the "psychological contract." The expectations of both employees and company are components of this. The parties to this contract may not themselves be aware of all the implications, but nevertheless their mutual expectations govern their relationships to each other. To achieve progress we should strive to make these relationships more rational, overt, and explicit.

It is true that we cannot begin to deal perfectly with all the exigencies and contingencies of organizational life, but the nagging thought persists that as considerable as our intellectual resources are, we should be able to arrange our organizational affairs far better than we do now. Perhaps in the process of achieving enlightened change in our occupational relationships, work may yet become a kind of worship. To the extent that we succeed in our efforts, the blight of avoidable absence may well diminish.

DISCUSSION

Panelists discussing the psychiatric aspects of absenteeism included Alfred Besunder, Esq., Director of the New York State Mental Health Department, Second Judicial Department, and Captain Patrick F. Carone, M.D., Department of Psychiatry, United States Army Hospital in Kentucky. Others were Louis R. Hott, M.D., Medical Director of the Karen Horney Clinic; Sherman N. Kieffer, M.D., Professor and Vice-Chairman of the Department of Psychiatry, Health Sciences Center, State University of New York at Stony Brook; and Sidney Merlis, M.D., Director of Psychiatric Research at Central Islip State Hospital. John MacIver, M.D., is Former Medical Director of the United States Steel Corporation, and Sidney Zuckerman, M.D., is Medical Director of the Sperry Division of the Sperry Rand Corporation.

Question:

How do you as a psychiatrist see the problem of absenteeism?

Dr. Merlis:

I am very much concerned about absenteeism in the research profession. The usual pattern of researchers is to work as they please, where they please, and when they please. In fact, history has shown that when a researcher is forced into a strict schedule, he becomes quite unproductive. In the present day and age, when we all must punch clocks and turn out so many items per day, it is very difficult to motivate researchers. I have noticed in many research operations, including my own, that there is a general decrease in morale. We cannot order researchers to think only between eight in the morning and four thirty in the afternoon with half an hour for lunch, yet labor unions and financial considerations are forcing us to do just that. In research fields today, we are finding significant problems in motivation and a great deal of unhappiness, which leads to absenteeism. It is time to stop measuring an individual's research productivity in terms of the number of papers he has written and instead give more emphasis to the quality of his work.

Mr. Besunder:

I am a director of a legal service which is involved with the constitutional rights of hospitalized individuals. I have noticed that while every member of this organization is entitled to thirteen days of sick leave per year, at the end of the year all of the younger employees have used up their allotted days while the older people or those in supervisory capacities tend to bank their sick leave. It appears that the older individuals have a greater awareness of the future.

Dr. Zuckerman:

There seems to be a difference, too, between the individual who is a junior executive or white collar worker or whose position is basically nonorganized and the blue collar worker whose job is more regimented. The individual who works at a desk and has certain duties knows very well that if he is absent, the work will pile up and he will have to get it done by staying late or taking the work home. If he does not do what is expected of him, he will probably lose his job. On the other hand, the employee who works at a machine knows that what he does not finish, the employee on the next shift will. It is very difficult to motivate such an individual, especially when he has the backing of a strong labor union. He is not particularly interested in doing a superior job nor in being present as often as he should.

This attitude is reflected in the rate of absenteeism or length of absence for any particular illness. Where the junior executive or clerk would take two or three days off from work for a cold, the average individual in a highly structured position would be out for two or three weeks.

Aside from the difficulty in firing the blue collar worker with union support, there is also the matter of money. With all of the benefits now offered to employees, the blue collar worker often does as well or better financially by not working as he does by going to work. It is possible that physicians are not particularly aware of what goes on in this regard. If doctors were more aware of the increase in cost of products by virtue of absenteeism, perhaps they would be more cautious in signing medical certificates.

Dr. Kieffer:

I feel that one of the most important things to be done is to dispel the notion that, as psychiatrists, we can come up with some sort of panacea for the absenteeism problem. We must stop discussing symptoms with the expectation that we are going to discover a magical cure for absenteeism or any other major problem. It is important to discuss absenteeism within a frame of reference and with respect to a goal, but if that goal is to be the complete eradication of the symptom, we will be deeply disappointed. If we set our sights somewhat lower and try to reattack and work on the preventive aspects of the problem, we will meet with much more success.

Dr. Hott:

I am directly concerned with industry and also work with patients in my office and at a clinic. In relation to my personal work with patients, I see a special kind of absenteeism. Many patients miss sessions even when they know they will have to pay for those missed sessions. When there is enough reason to miss a session, not necessarily a conscious reason, we call it resistance or inability to face many problems.

Another aspect of absenteeism involves not only a psychological but a sociological concept. Not only is today's society extremely competitive, but it is also mechanized and specialized; as a result, it produces a certain type of reaction, even a certain type of structured personality. In other words, we become dependent. One of the things we become dependent upon is the work we do or the company with which we are associated. This dependency often conflicts with the individual's other feelings about his job or company, such as hostility, aggression, or a search for achievement and independence. This conflict may produce many kinds of difficulty, depending upon how the individual is able to deal with the conflict and his anxiety. Emotional problems and psychosomatic illnesses may result, and these lead to absenteeism. In addition, there are unconscious motivations in the individual to be absent. Years ago, we found a great deal of "Sunday neurosis": people who were somehow "addicted" to work and who became ill only on weekends. Today we see the opposite phenomenon.

Dr. Carone:

We have talked about absenteeism and presenteeism, but we have not discussed the individual who is physically at work but who is not there in terms of his emotional or motivational attitudes. An individual who has very little choice as to whether or not he will do a certain job and who does not want to do the job shows a certain pattern of behavior. He will do the absolute minimum expected of him in the worst possible way he can. This attitude touches on what Dr. Hott was focusing on: the passive-dependent, passive-aggressive style of relating. The individual has to do a certain job but hates the thought of it. He does as poor a job as possible, perhaps as a way of trying to sabotage things. In many cases, this is not at all unconscious. I feel that this situation is a precursor of absenteeism.

Something else which possibly leads to absenteeism is the tendency of management and high level union leaders to make workers into duplicates of themselves: aggressive, achievement and prestige-oriented, and money-oriented. Not all people are highly motivated to achieve, and these efforts of management could add an additional source of conflict to already troubled employees. The leaders of industry should recognize that not all individuals have the same values and goals.

Question:

Isn't the situation actually that high level management does not want employees to be duplicates of themselves? Wouldn't management be threatened by aggressive, creative employees?

Dr. Hott:

I feel that management does want its employees to be achievement-oriented, particularly in terms of profits. But when employees do show these leadership qualities, management is often threatened and shows ambivalence. This is where the conflict is.

Audience:

Perhaps what industrial leaders are striving for is a factory full of enthusiastic, production-oriented employees who generate much in the way of profits. But these same employees must not be aggressive or achievement-oriented in terms of threatening and taking the place of these very human industrial leaders.

Question:

Do you consider absenteeism something that can be treated by a psychiatrist?

Dr. Hott:

What is important is the motivation behind the decision to be absent. If an individual is compulsively driven to work, I would say that this is not a healthy individual. If an individual is compulsively driven to stay away from work, this is also unhealthy. However, if an individual is truly able to make a free choice and decides that he does not want to work, I would say that this is healthy, as long as he hurts neither himself nor society by his decision.

Audience:

My own experience is that young people in particular are disillusioned by what they see of work. They see an employee who has worked for fifty years receive a gold watch and retire. They would wonder what the point is, what they will get out of working.

Mr. Besunder:

In trying to formulate an opinion on why people work and why they are absent, I thought of professional athletes and the tremendous salaries that many of them receive. I would venture to say that their rate of absenteeism is minimal. If their legs are in casts or their arms are wrapped in bandages, they continue to play. I wondered whether the primary factor is the financial remuneration or whether it is the ego boost these individuals receive from all the publicity.

Maybe we should try to motivate employees in a similar way. Industries could publish newspapers filled with the achievements of individual factories or employees.

Question:

What is the crux of the absenteeism problem as seen by the psychiatrist?

Dr. Hott:

We often hear people put a value judgment on absenteeism of a certain type. That is, absenteeism is considered acceptable and justified when an individual is "sick." This is where the problem lies. It is not a question of whether something is justifiable or not. It is a question of really analyzing what is happening. For instance, an individual may find himself in the midst of a conflict. He has dependency needs and wants to be taken care of; at the same time, he needs to be an independent adult and hold onto his job. He may be torn between his desires to assert himself and his needs to be told what to do. Depending upon how strong the conflict is and depending upon how the individual handles his opposing needs, he may develop a psychosis, a cold, heart disease, or nothing at all. If he is sick, he certainly has a right to be sick, but we can help him if we are able to understand what made him sick.

Question:

How can we handle absenteeism, and how effective can we be?

Dr. Hott:

I have found the team approach to be quite effective. If employees are grouped together on production teams, and the teams compete with one another, absenteeism drops and employees want to stay at work. They are being motivated not only by money, but by their innate competitiveness as enhanced in this setting. There is nothing wrong with competitiveness. The important point is how we deal with it.

Audience:

The Gallup Poll has shown that money motivates people more

than anything else. In addition, various organizations have shown that rewards for good attendance records have helped to decrease rates of absenteeism. The significance of these decreases suggests that there is real potential in job manipulation or reward manipulation. I wonder, however, whether these positive findings are merely short-term results. Is it not possible that there might be negative aspects to so inducing people to come to work when, in fact, it might be healthier to leave them with a simple choice of whether or not to come in? In the long run, this could have a negative effect.

Dr. MacIver:

What you have implied is that people should have an internalized investment in their jobs. This is what really counts, rather than their having to be manipulated by external contingencies. These reward manipulations have a carrot and stick aspect and really diminish motivation and morale *and* productivity.

Question:

What are we going to recommend to industry as a way of coping effectively with the habitually absent individual who is demonstrating a character or neurotic disturbance?

Dr. Carone:

To my knowledge, psychiatric treatment of the character disorder, the individual who acts on impulse and does not plan for long range goals, is not particularly successful in the military, in private practice, or in industry.

Question:

Are problems of dependency found on the executive levels of an organization as well as on the lower levels?

Dr. Hott:

Dependency does not refer only to the lower echelon of an organization. It is well known that the highest rate of peptic ulcers is found in executives. On the surface, these high-achieving individuals appear very aggressive, independent, and hard-driving. Yet underneath they are extremely dependent, and herein lies the conflict that leads to such things as ulcers. Dependency is found on every level of an organization. However, the higher one goes, the less he is allowed to feel or admit to his dependency. He must be independent.

Question:

Is there any correlation between an individual's record of school attendance and his work attendance?

Audience:

There is a very definite correlation. Those people who are guilty of absenteeism in school are also guilty of absenteeism later on in life. The syndrome is almost incurable. The only way for the employer to defend against this kind of person is for the employer to carefully investigate school records and other attendance records before hiring an individual.

Question:

It has been said that 10 percent of employees are responsible for 90 percent of the absenteeism in industry. Why should we focus on a relatively small percentage of people who are responsible for most of the problems?

Dr. Carone:

This relates to group pathology. We are seeing the symptomatology of a whole sick group expressed through a minority of the members of the group. This is why these individuals demand our attention and why it is imperative that we give them our attention.

PUBLIC HEALTH ASPECTS OF ABSENTEEISM IN INDUSTRY: THE NATIONAL VIEWPOINT

JESSE L. STEINFELD*

H EALTH PROBLEMS in the United States today are largely man's own creation. In past centuries infectious diseases, problems of nutrition, trauma, and natural disasters, have been the source of man's illnesses. In more recent years, technogenic diseases, that is, those diseases resulting from man's use of technology, are accounting for more and more of our problems. A technogenic disease would be one which was not anticipated but which resulted from man's use of technology.

In a very real sense all of our occupational diseases and all instances of drug abuse, including alcoholic abuse, are technogenic diseases. Even the iatrogenic diseases are a special example of technogenic disease. Iatrogenic diseases are those caused by the physician's use of an agent which produces an unexpected illness in the patient. Technogenic diseases result from man's increasing use of technology to solve not only medical but other problems as well; as we conquer the infectious, nutritional, and metabolic diseases, our largest health problems in the form of psychological or physical diseases result from man's own activity.

Many members of our society, especially those in the legislative and executive branches of government, are now concerned with

---

*Jesse L. Steinfeld, M.D. has had a distinguished career in medicine and public service. He has been Professor of Medicine at the University of Southern California, following which he became Associate Director of the National Cancer Institute and, later, Deputy Director. Doctor Steinfeld most recently was Surgeon General of the United States and now is the Chairman of the Department of Oncology at the Mayo Clinic.

technology assessment, but we have no valid techniques for gauging the results of our technological expertise. If we are to avoid major problems in the future, we must begin to expend a significant fraction of the energy and resources in technology assessment as we expend on technology. This is clearly a major challenge for the future in all the industrialized nations.

Several years ago, an extensive review of the hundreds of health programs within the Department of Health, Education, and Welfare was undertaken. In that review a phenomenon was uncovered which directly relates to the success or failure of a number of our health programs, both present and past. Where the American citizen is passive, programs are generally successful. That is, where we purify water, collect garbage, develop vaccines, immunize the population, and pasteurize milk, our programs are eminently successful. Our society fails, however, when the citizens must take a continuing, active role for himself: where he must stop smoking, not abuse alcohol, not drive after drinking, use sane nutritional principles, and exercise. When an American citizen is required to take an active and continuing role in his own behalf, he refuses. There is a lesson here for industry and employees: either we try to develop programs in which the worker can be passive or we learn about motivational techniques to determine which kinds of programs our citizens can be motivated enough to undertake.

As a background for discussion of absenteeism in industry, I will review some of our national statistics.

There are two elementary and essential functions served by statistics in our society. First, they provide quantitative evidence of the existence of problems; and second, they mark progress or lack of progress in dealing with these problems. Alternatively, statistics may simply place a supposition on a firm basis and add a measure of magnitude.

The lowest rates for infant mortality are in the suburban counties outside of large metropolitan areas. The highest rates are in the urban ghettoes. Although the United States lags behind a number of industrialized countries in terms of maternal mortality, there has been a dramatic decline in maternal mortality, particularly in the minority racial groups, over the last one or two decades;

nonetheless, the rates still have not reached the level of the white population. In fact, whether or not maternal mortality is high or low in the United States depends more on economics than on racial make-up.

In reviewing death rates, there is an excess in minority group mortality throughout the list of the major causes of death in this country. There are especially great discrepancies in tuberculosis and other infectious and parasitic diseases. The most dramatic difference between the non-white and white populations, however, is in the incidence of homicide. The only disease in which the white population has a higher adjusted death rate is chronic respiratory diseases. In infant mortality, we find that those infants who weigh 2500 grams or less and are from low income groups have a significantly higher mortality. This may relate to cigarette smoking in that women who smoke cigarettes during the latter two trimesters of pregnancy have a significantly higher incidence of infants weighing under 2500 grams and, therefore, higher neonatal mortality.

We know that individuals from different economic and ethnic backgrounds see physicians and dentists at a different rate, the white population sees dentists more frequently. The difference is quite striking across income groups. While it is still much more likely that a white individual or family will have seen a dentist in the last year, with the advent of Medicare and Medicaid, the days and number of physician visits is practically the same across the economic spectrum. There is also a difference in the long-term mental hospitalization rate by individuals in terms of both geographic region and race. There is a higher proportionate black population in mental institutions, particularly in the South. Finally, there is a difference in the number of physicians available to various population groups, again depending upon the median income in the area. Those areas that have a higher median income have more physicians immediately available.

With these data as background, let us turn to data from the latest National Health Survey on Absenteeism. First, I will describe the source of the data and some of its limitations, indicating wherein our health interview data differ from those collected by the Department of Labor. Then I will review the labor force and discuss time lost from work overall and, more specifically, from work injuries. Finally, I will comment on chronic activity limitations and alcoholism.

The National Health Survey was established by Congress in 1956. The Health Interview Survey, which was the first in a family of several different survey mechanisms, begun in 1957 and is conducted by a group within the Public Health Service called the National Center for Health Statistics. The data are collected under contract with the Bureau of Census from a sample of 42,000 households representing the civilian, noninstitutionalized population of the United States. Sampling is spread throughout the year to reduce any seasonal bias. The census interviewers have no special medical training and they collect data about all members of the family on a structured questionnaire. One half to three quarters of an hour are required for the interview, and information is obtained from any responsible adult present at the time of the interview, usually the wife or mother. Only about 40 percent of the data are obtained directly from the male of the family. The information is collected on 135,000 persons each year.

Interviewers collect data on a wide variety of conditions: acute, chronic, restricted activity days, bed days, work loss days, long-term limitation of activity, utilization of physicians, and so forth. In addition, there are specific questions each year, such as health insurance coverage, smoking habits, exposure to X-ray, and who pays for the medical service. The data are then extrapolated to provide estimates for the total civilian noninstitutionalized population and are published in a number of different reports.

The information obtained on chronic and acute conditions is limited by the extent to which respondents can provide accurate diagnostic information about their conditions; frequently, patients are not good sources of medical data, so one must look at these data with that in mind. For purposes of definition, conditions are considered chronic if they have been in existence during the twelve months before the interview and lasted at least three months.

It will be helpful to be aware of some additional limitations. As I mentioned, data collected on chronic and acute conditions are coded to the international classification of diseases, but the amount of diagnostic detail which is available is limited by the extent to which the respondent is willing and able to convey this type of information to an interviewer. People usually do not talk about venereal disease, alcoholism, or drug abuse.

The data obtained from an interview is much different from that obtained from other public health sources or from physicians. The respondent may be aware of a condition. However, he may not wish to discuss his problem with a stranger who comes to the door with a half-hour questionnaire. Thus, as a result of these limitations, data from a household interview survey will differ from data derived from medical records. In general, interview data are limited to those illnesses and diseases of which respondents are aware and which they are willing to talk about. These are also the conditions which are most related to their health care utilization and behavior. While the sample is large in comparison to most surveys, it is still inadequate for making estimates of realatively rare types of health events. For example, a survey cannot provide estimates of detailed types of occupational accidents or injuries or occupationally related diseases, such as specific types of pneumococci. Special studies of select population groups are needed to obtain data on these relatively rare events.

The definitions of work loss used by the Health Interview Survey should be clearly understood when considering the data presented later. A day of work loss is one in which a currently employed person is absent from his job for all or most of his regular hours as a result of illness or injury. This definition is different from that used by the Bureau of Labor Statistics in that the Bureau counts only full days lost following the day of the injury while the Health group counts the day of the injury as a work loss day.

Work loss, however, can be due to other than occupationally related illnesses or injuries and, in fact, less than half of them are related to occupational injury. One type of absenteeism that is not generally included in the data from the Health Interview Survey is work loss due to pregnancy. In the first place, pregnancy is not classified as an illness. Thus, a person on routine maternity leave would not be included in the work loss estimate; our estimates comparing work loss levels of males and females, then, are misleading to the extent that they exclude the majority of maternity leave.

Another related problem is that work loss figures are only for persons who are currently employed; many pregnant females actually drop out of the labor force during preganancy and, therefore, would not be included in work loss estimates, even if pregnancy were considered an illness. In the future, we are going to collect additional information regarding pragnancy.

A final limitation of the work loss data from the interview survey is that it is only for work loss due to illness or injury of the employed person. The estimates do not include absenteeism when a man has to stay home to care for a sick wife or if a mother loses time to take her sick child to the doctor. Work loss days do not include times lost from work for preventive health care such as annual physician examinations or reporting for immunizations. Once again, we are now developing a new set of questions to be used in the future; hopefully, these will determine the amount of time lost from work because of illness in other family members and also time lost for preventive health care. In addition, these same plans include attempting to measure the amount of income lost as a result of illness, both for the worker and for other members of the family. As we gain more and more experience in these areas, we will be able to obtain more refined data.

During 1971, an estimated 41.1 percent of the civilian, non-institutionalized population of two hundred two million people reported themselves as members of the working force. Of these, 83,-077,000, or 93 percent, reported that they were currently employed: worked at some time during the two-week period prior to the interview, had a job, or owned a business. (This description of the labor force is based on data from the Health Interview Survey and differs from the official Bureau of Labor Statistics.)

About six of each ten currently employed persons are males, and the same proportion were in the age group seventeen years to forty-four years. About one third were in the forty-five to sixty-four years age bracket, and the remaining 4 percent were over age sixty-five. Seven of every ten currently employed persons work within three industry groups: manufacturing with nineteen million;

wholesale and retail trade, fifteen million; and services with twenty million, five hundred thousand. In the last decade, services have overtaken the manufacturing industries in terms of numbers of employed persons.

In terms of time lost from work, 77.4 million currently employed persons reported losing about four hundred million days from work because of illness or injury during 1971. This is an average of 5.1 days lost per worker. Female workers reported an average of 5.5 days while males reported an average of 4.9 days. The sex difference in time lost from work occurred primarily among workers under forty-five years of age. For example, females between the ages of seventeen and twenty-four years lost 4.8 days while males that age lost only 3.8 days. Females twenty-five to forty-four years lost one day more than their male counterparts. For workers between the ages of forty-five and sixty-four years, however, males and females showed the same average number of days lost from work; among workers over sixty-five years, females lost fewer work days than males. The sex difference for work days lost appears as one moves into the postmenopausal age group. For all currently employed persons, the rate of work loss days was highest for people forty-five to sixty-four years at 6.1 days as compared to 4.2 days for employees in the seventeen to twenty-four age group.

The rate of work loss days varies considerably depending upon family income. The combined family income, of course, is different from the individual income. The number of days lost from work was highest among persons whose family income was lowest. Thus, the 4.4 million persons with income under $3,000 per year lost 9.4 days from work whereas those with a family income over $15,000 lost only four days. In addition, there is a variation depending upon place of residence and geographic region. Those in metropolitan areas lose more days, 5.3, as contrasted with those who live on farms, 4.5 days. In the South, there is a somewhat higher rate, 5.5 days, as compared to 4.8 days in the North and Central regions. White individuals in the currently employed population reported 4.8 days lost from work as compared with 7.5 days for the non-white population.

If we look at the various industry groups, we find some interesting differences. The relatively small number of individuals in mining, about five hundred thousand, lost an average of 8.8 days; the next highest rate was for the manufacturing industries, where an average of 6.2 days were lost per employee. The farmers probably had the lowest rate of loss for any single occupational group.

Insofar as reasons for absences, about 262 million of the 400 million days lost were lost as a result of acute conditions. Those would include respiratory illnesses, which account for half of the work loss due to acute conditions. Injuries caused about one day lost from work per person per year; therefore, acute respiratory disease and injuries caused seven of every ten days lost from work. If we assume that currently employed individuals had no more than one acute illness or injury on the same day during the year, then it may be considered that the 134 million days not accounted for by acute conditions were caused by chronic diseases. Thus, of the 5.1 days lost for all reasons, 3.4 were due to acute and 1.7 due to chronic conditions.

Work injuries are highest among the blue collar workers. While they comprise 37 percent of the currently employed population, blue collar workers accounted for 72 percent of all of the injuries during the year, which had a significant impact upon disability. Injuries sustained at work accounted for 47 percent of the restricted activity days, 44 percent of the injury induced bed disability days, and 52 percent of the work loss days. Of all blue collar workers injured on the job, 94 percent were males between the ages of seventeen and sixty-four years; that is, virtually all injuries were accounted for by the male working population. In addition, the summary findings are that laborers had significantly higher rates of restricted activity days, bed disability days, and work loss days. Older workers experience substantially more days in these three categories, as well. The male blue collar workers in the West had the highest rates of work injuries, while white persons sustained approximately half the bed disability days and substantially smaller rates of restricted activity in work than the blue collar workers who were non-white. Furthermore, higher rates of restricted activity and work loss are found with the less educated blue collar workers.

In 1970, for the first time, the Health Interview Survey collected data on cigarette smoking. It was found that cigarette smokers experience 45 percent more days lost from work due to illness and injury than people who never smoke cigarettes. Cigarette smokers lose on the average 6.3 days per year while persons who never smoke lose 4.4 days. The same pattern holds for both males and females. Females, who show a lesser rate of bronchogenic carcinoma and coronary occlusions associated with smoking, nonetheless have the same proportionate increase in days lost from work as compared with the non-smoking females. Former smokers tend to report more work loss due to illness than those who never smoked, but less work lost than present cigarette smokers. There is also a higher proportion of cigarette mokers among the currently employed population than the general population; about 42 percent of the currently employed smoke, whereas only 37 percent of the total population are considered current cigarette smokers.

Among males, blue collar workers have the highest proportion of cigarette smokers at 53 percent while farm workers show the lowest rate, 34 percent. The largest group of former smokers are white collar males at 30 percent. Within that group, doctors probably account for many of the former smokers in the country.

Again, the National Health Survey data contain only that information which interviewees volunteer. Work absence due to alcoholism or simple desire not to go to work will not be found in this data. The recently established National Institute of Alcohol Abuse and Alcoholism estimates that 5 percent of the nation's work force and possibly 10 percent of executives have alcohol abuse related problems. We estimate problem drinkers at 4.5 million.

When we reviewed this problem in government three years ago, we found possibly the most unenlightened policies of any industry. Alcoholism was considered a reason for discharge. Before we could mount any kind of national program, it was necessary for the government to change its attitudes and its rules and regulations regarding alcohol abuse and what can be done about it once it is discovered.

At this time, over three hundred private corporations have implemented programs designed to detect, treat, and, hopefully, to prevent end stage alcoholism. The most successful programs in industry and government aim at the entire spectrum of behavioral problems rather than focus on the end stage alcoholic. Organized labor, too, is lending its efforts toward the same preventive and therapeutic goal. The more successful industrial programs have a 50 percent to 70 percent rate of improvement when the alcohol abuser is identified early, his physical health has not deteriorated, his financial recources are not depleted, and he still has the emotional support of his family, community, and place of work. In addition, his motivation for recovery is still quite strong. These are the elements which make for a successful program.

According to our most recent estimates, 50 percent of our nation's alcoholics are currently employed. Not only do they create problems for themselves and their fellow employees, but they are absent two and one-half times as often as the non-alcoholic employees. The total cost to the nation from immoderate drinking is fifteen billion dollars per year, of which about ten billion represents the employer's loss, two billion goes toward health and welfare services, and three billon for property damage, insurance expenses, medical expenses, and wage losses.

As we look at the rest of the decade of the seventies and toward the eighties, what are the likely changes in the health care system in the United States? First, it is obvious that government will become more and more involved, even with the current retrenchment. The number of bills pending before Congress indicates that there will be greater and greater involvement of government in the health care system. In my discussions with health leaders of other nations, I have repeatedly heard the advice that we should embark on large scale experiments in health care delivery in order to avoid the kinds of mistakes they have made when they have attempted to blanket their entire nation with some preconceived idea which had not been tested.

The industrial medical sector in particular in the United States has an opportunity to begin preventive programs, screening programs, and therapeutic programs as well as to relate more closely to the family, the private physician, and the private hospital. Here, attempts can be made to develop new types of systems which, while they may not be applicable throughout the country, may be applicable in some geographic, economic, or employment regions. Above all, the important thing is to begin thinking about ways in which we might do more than we are doing. We must look at what needs to be done in term of our society's health needs and utilize some of the inexpensive chemical screening devices and computer-automated history procedures.

In conclusion, our health care system is undergoing a great deal of needed change, and the industrial medical sector can be an extremely important part of this change. By expending more effort in preventive medicine, industrial medicine has an opportunity to reduce not only absenteeism, but all related problems.

DISCUSSION

Chairman of this panel was Jesse L. Steinfeld, M.D., Surgeon General, United States Department of Health, Education and Welfare. Panelists were individuals very much involved in the day-to-day aspects of absenteeism. These included Henry Brill, M.D., Director of Pilgrim State Hospital and Robert E. Fishbein, M.D., Medical Director of the Sperry Rand Corporation. Edward Malone, M.D., is Clinical Director of South Oaks Hospital, Amityville, New York. Others were Robert J. Oehrig, M.D., Medical Director of Home Life Insurance Company of New York and Harry E. Tebrock, M.D., Medical Director of General Telephone and Electronics Corporation.

Dr. Brill:

In my own experience as a mental hospital administrator I find that not showing up for scheduled work is steadily increasing. Economic and social factors are probably as important as the interacting psychiatric factors in contributing to absenteeism. One of the most prominent is the practice of "moonlighting"; many people actually hold two full-time jobs and are simply unable to keep up with both. There is another form of the two job syndrome; this is the case of the working woman who also has a family and home to take care of. Under these pressures, a great deal of absenteeism results, and much of it is not scattered randomly but is concentrated at certain times, especially weekends, holidays, and school vacation periods.

Perhaps it would help to classify absenteeism into various types and deal with each separately. Alcoholism has been perhaps the most publicized cause of absenteeism, and drug abuse has recently become prominent, but there are many others, and many factors interact. Each type may have certain external characteristics that could help identify it. For example, the alcoholic is traditionally away from work one day at a time: Monday. The drug dependent individual on the other hand is likely to be away for longer and more irregular blocks of time. This entire subject deserves more study than it has had. It is certainly a major problem in the health industry as I know it. It becomes increasingly difficult to deliver medical care in a hospital where service must be continuous and yet large proportions of the staff do not show up for work at certain times.

Dr. Fishbein:

When dealing with absenteeism, it is often helpful to establish a performance pattern for any particular individual. This is the job of the personnel department and possibly the medical department.

An individual may not have any alcohol or drug related problems, but there are other stressful situations such as family problems which can result in absenteeism. Sometimes these problems can be resolved with the help of the personnel or medical department. The company has the choice of taking a cold, hard-line approach: "Either straighten out or lose your job," or taking a more flexible, "meet you half-way" approach. Companies also have the option of using a motivation incentive approach to reduce absenteeism. This involves paying employees for perfect attendance records.

Dr. Malone:

The Dean of Harvard College once made a remark to the effect that the primary duty of a college is to encourage students to make some sort of a commitment. This also has some bearing on how people feel about work. Whether or not an industrial corporation is in the position of trying to get workers to make commitments seems irrelevant, since it is a little too late at that point.

In any event, work is not necessarily a primary commitment

for many young people today. Recreational activities are their primary commitments, and work becomes secondary. The job itself may be a significant factor in this lack of commitment, particularly if the task is tedious and repetitive. However, I feel that the lack of commitment really relates back to the value placed on work in our general society.

Dr. Oehrig:

I am interested in the other side of the coin. I find myself extremely pleased with the number of employees who do come in to work out of a sense of loyalty and responsibility when they may not really be up to it physically. This is not restricted to the older employees who have been with the company for twenty years or longer. We find a good bit of this phenomenon in people who have been with the company less than five years.

These people come in because, first of all, they are needed. Second, they clearly have some sense of fulfillment in their jobs; they are not bored, they have a sense of personal worth in what they are doing and finally, they recognize that their work is important in the functioning of their section or department.

In terms of absenteeism, however, it is interesting to differentiate between the reasons for the short, one or two-day absence, and the longer absence lasting a week or more. The long absence is due to disability of some kind; cardiovascular and gastrointestinal problems are most prevalent. The occasional (or frequent) one or two-day absentees are the poorly motivated employees, the alcoholics, and perhaps the drug users.

My final comment has to do with the variability in absence rates according to the size of the company. It is not too surprising that in studies made elsewhere, a giant corporation has a higher absence rate than a company of five hundred employees. It is very interesting, however, and unexplained so far, that the very small company generally has a poorer rate of attendance than the intermediate-sized company.

Dr. Tebrock:

I represent a very large industry with employees not only throughout the United States, but scattered around the world.

We are a utility as well as a manufacturing group. It is amazing to see the difference in absentee rates in our utilities section as opposed to our manufacturing group. In addition, there is a definite geographically variability in absenteeism.

For instance, in Belgium we have very little absenteeism. We do not find the Monday or Friday absentee which we all ascribe to the alcoholic. In Belgium, the law requires that we have a bar in each factory where wine, beer, brandy, and vermouth are served. As a result, the factory becomes a very social place, and people enjoy coming to work.

Question:
What is the accident rate like?

Dr. Tebrock:
The accident rate in factories with bars is no greater than that in factories in other countries without alcohol served during the day.

In Brazil, the employees have two hours for lunch, during which time they are free to visit the local bars. However, we do not have the accident rate or the absenteeism in Brazil that we have in California. Our largest telephone company is in California and employs many individuals such as installers who are required to be on their own all day. Consequently, it is very difficult for the supervisor to keep track of these employees. If these individuals go to a bar for a few hours in the middle of the day and then go back to work until dark, accidents are almost inevitable, particularly when these men are working on top of telephone poles.

In Japan, we have no problem at all. The Japanese government subsidizes industry in many cases, and as a result, an attitude of loyalty to employer and government has been established in the Japanese employee.

Even within the United States there is a great deal of geographic variability in absence rates. In a small state like Idaho, there is a minimum of absenteeism because individuals need jobs and there are very few choices. If an employee in Idaho loses his job with a large corporation, he may not have anyplace else to go. There is necessarily a great deal of company loyalty.

The situation in New York City, Los Angeles, and Chicago is entirely different. Many different kinds of people with widely varying attitudes and many options available are found in these metropolitan areas. Here, job loyalty is not so important a factor.

The place for industrial medicine today is not only in the preventive area, but also in the therapeutic area. However, industry cannot undertake the delivery of health services alone. Labor unions and government must come together with management to bring to American public a better system of health care delivery.

Dr. Steinfeld:

It is important to differentiate between the individual who should not be absent and the one who is genuinely sick but whose illness or accident could have been prevented by utilizing appropriate medical and/or industrial safeguards.

Another point I would like to make concerns instances when employees leave their jobs to take children to the dentist or physician. We really have not made use of our school systems. Preventive dentistry, for instance, could ideally be handled in schools if the equipment were there. Many activities that we ordinarily consider the private practice of medicine or dentistry could probably be carried out in places where the population is not necessarily captive but where there would be a minimal amount of time lost in travel.

Dr. Tebrock:

It is important to recognize that both tobacco and drug addiction contribute to absenteeism. However, the major problem for industry remains alcoholism. It is only recently that the average industry formulated a policy regarding alcoholism. Not more than a decade ago, the average industry immediately fired and discarded the alcoholic employee.

Now we have changed our attitude, primarily because some enlightened management along with government and medical agencies have discovered that alcoholism is a treatable disease. The prevalent policy today is not to fire the alcoholic, but to find him before he becomes hopeless and before he becomes a director or a supervisor. We must educate our employees. In the past, supervisors have been the greatest deterrent to finding and helping alcoholics because supervisors often believe they are doing the kind thing by covering up an employee's drinking problem. Alcoholism contributes greatly to absenteeism, and getting to the heart of the matter requires education, reeducation, and exposure.

Question:

How widespread is this change in attitude toward the alcoholic on the part of management? Is not the alcoholic still more likely to be fired when exposed?

Dr. Tebrock:

Unfortunately, yes. The attitude change has been most profound in the largest industries, those which have the benefit of large and enlightened medical departments.

Audience:

A recent study found only twelve companies out of one and one-half million corporations in this country to have adequate and workable alcoholism programs.

Audience:

In speaking with young people, I have found this next generation of workers to be both cynical and ignorant of the dangers of tobacco, alcohol, and other drugs. Do you have any plans for mandatory alcohol education?

Dr. Steinfeld:

I feel that rather than have the school football coach casually teach health education classes, this area is important enough that we should license educators in the health fields. A good hygiene textbook is needed, and a comprehensive curriculum must be developed. Unless we start such a program, we are going to be faced with another generation of employees who are prone to alcoholism, drug abuse, and absenteeism.

Dr. Brill:

I think that it is possible to overvalue the effect of information alone. There is a distinct need for motivation. The medical profession knows all about alcohol, drugs, and suicide, yet the rates of these three problems among the medical profession compete with those of any other group in society.

Dr. Steinfeld:

We really do not know how to motivate people with information alone. Perhaps we are providing it improperly. We need techniques to motivate people to both seek out and utilize the information which we currently have available. I try to distinguish health information from health education. The health educated person *acts* on the basis of the health information he has.

Dr. Malone:

It is my feeling that good health is not of primary value to young people in comparison with such things as sexual and athletic prowess.

Dr. Steinfeld:

It is only when people are in ill health that good health becomes a desideratum. This is, unfortunately, a fact of life, and its effects on absenteeism are seen every day. Only with the combined efforts of management, labor, government, and the medical professions can we hope to find a solution.

INDEX

education in human relations, 46
responsibilities of, 25-26
Supervisor training, 7, 10, 55-56, 65
Sweisgood, P., 10

T

Tebrock, H.E., 124
Technogenic disease, 114
Technology assessment, concern with, 114-115

Tobacco addiction, 122, 128
Transportation, problems of, 8

W

Walker, G.I., 28
Waters, E., 88
Weiss, H.R., 10
Whitehouse, F.A., 47
Worker unrest, manifestation of, 23

Z

Zuckerman, S., 106